THANET - CANTERBUR

HERNE BAY · SANDWICH · WHITSTABLE

G000117531

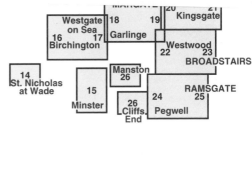

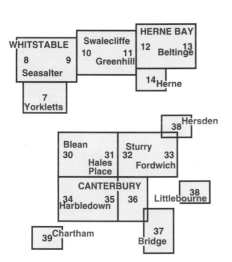

MARGATE 20 21 Kingsgate
Westgate 18 19
on Sea Garlinge
16 17
Birchington Westwood
22 23
14 BROADSTAIRS
St. Nicholas Manston
at Wade 26
15 24 25 RAMSGATE
Minster 26
Cliffs, Pegwell
End

WHITSTABLE Swalecliffe HERNE BAY
10 11 12 13
8 9 Greenhill Beltinge
Seasalter
14 Herne
7
Yorkletts

38 Hersden

Blean Sturry
30 31 32 33
Hales Fordwich
Place
CANTERBURY
34 35 36 38 Littlebourne
Harbledown
39 Chartham 37
Bridge

Ash 27
28 29 SANDWICH
Woodnesborough
27 Eastry

Every effort has been made to verify the accuracy of information in this book but the publishers cannot accept responsibility for expense or loss caused by an error or omission. Information that will be of assistance to the user of the maps will be welcomed.

The representation on these maps of a road, track or path is no evidence of the existence of a right of way.

Car Park	P
Public Convenience	C
Place of Worship	+
One-way Street	→
Pedestrianized	▨
Post Office	●

Scale of street plans 4 inches to 1 mile
Unless otherwise stated

Street plans prepared and published by ESTATE PUBLICATIONS, Bridewell House, TENTERDEN, KENT, and based upon the ORDNANCE SURVEY mapping with the permission of The Controller of H. M. Stationery Office.

The Publishers acknowledge the co-operation of the local authorities of towns represented in this atlas.

© Estate Publications 040 M   ISBN 0 86084 894 9   © Crown Copyright 398713

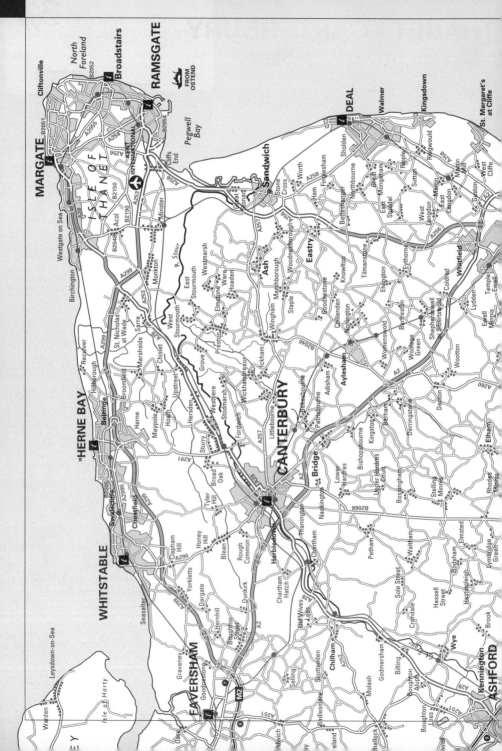

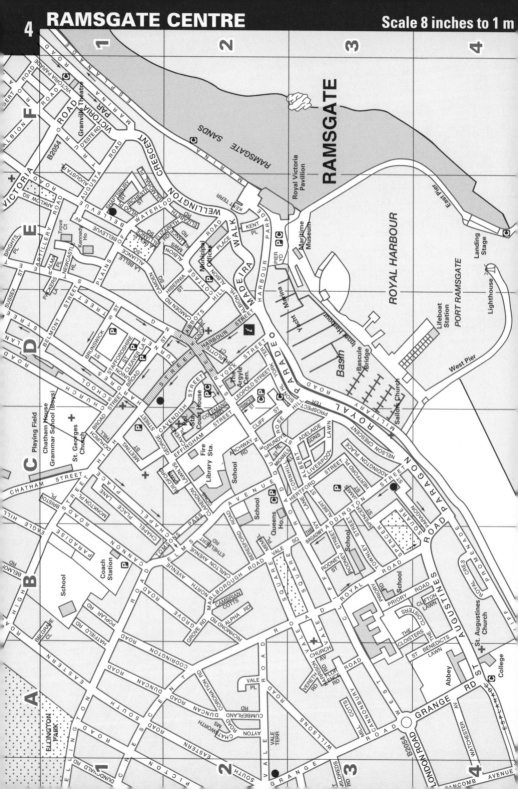

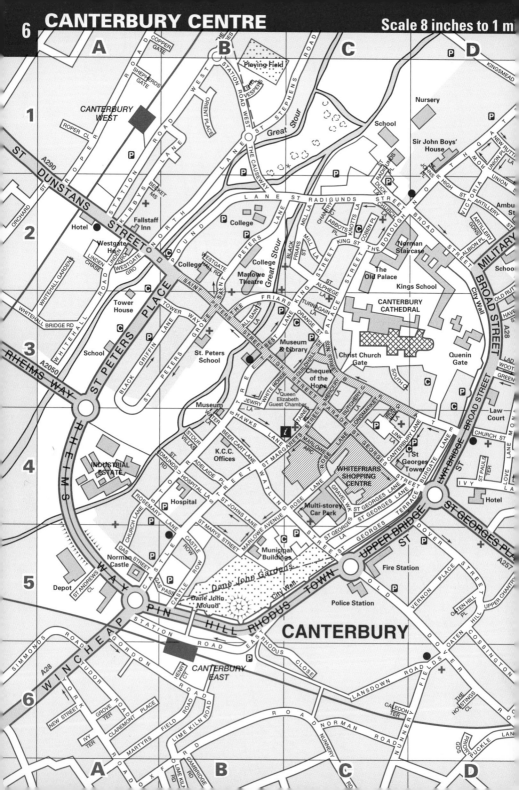

Yorkletts

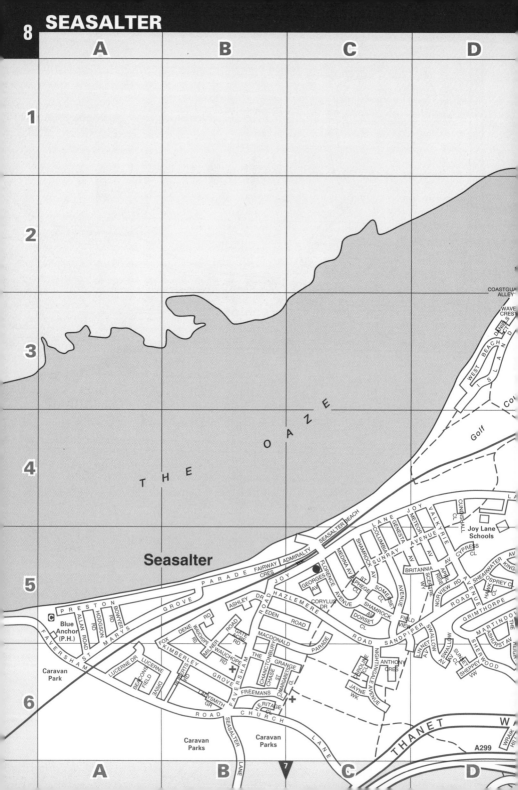

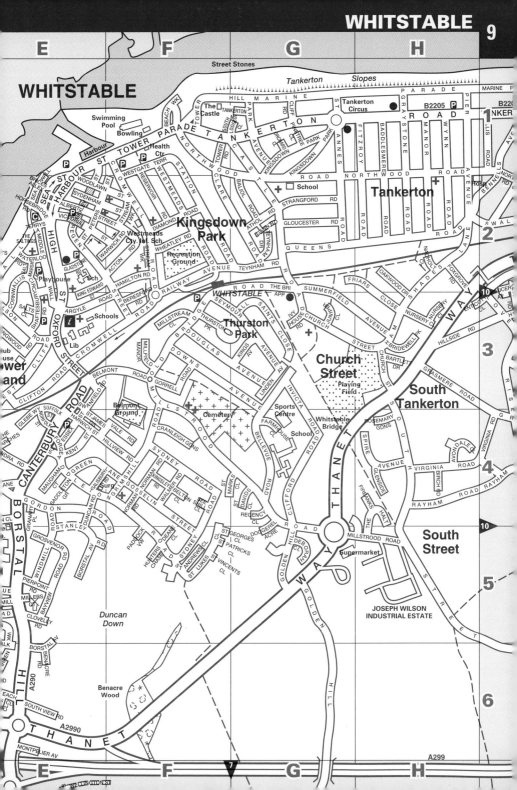

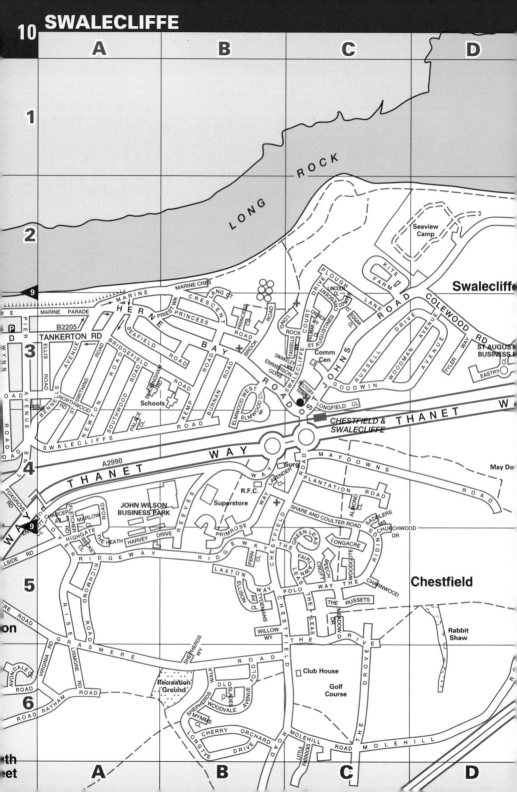

SWALECLIFFE

Chestfield

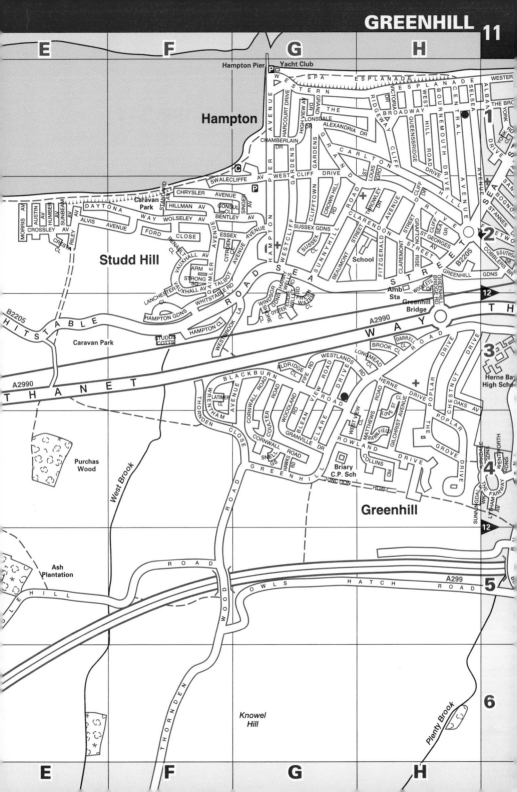

E   F   G   H

Hampton Pier   Yacht Club

Hampton

Studd Hill

Caravan Park

Caravan Park

Purchas Wood

West Brook

Ash Plantation

Knowel Hill

Greenhill

Briary C.P. Sch

Briary School

Herne Bay High Sch

Plenty Brook

1
2
3
4
5
6

E   F   G   H

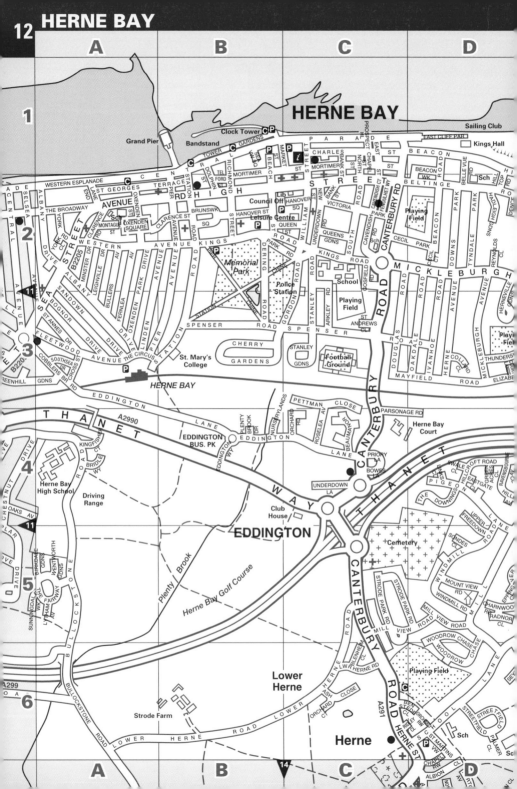

E F G H

Beltinge Cliff

Bishopstone

Caravan
Site

Beltinge

Bogshole
Bridge

Blacksole
Bridge

Broomfield

T H A N E T   W A Y

A299

**Hunters
Forstal**

Camping
Site

Hawe
Farm

1

2

3

4

5

6

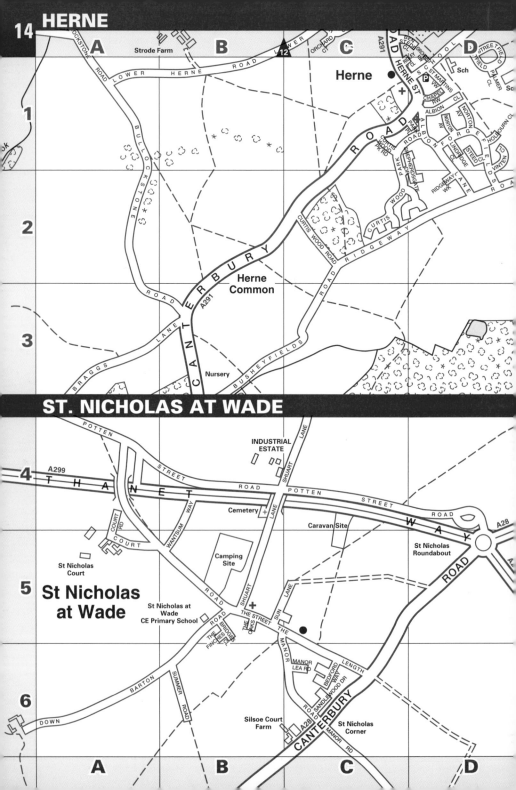

A   **B**   **C**   **D**

Cheeseman Farm

UMSTONE

B2048

MINSTER ROAD

Acol

Cleve Court Farm

MANSTON PARK

Alland Grange

MANSTON PARK

COLUM BUS AV

COLUM BUS AV

OLD MINSTER ROAD

MINSTER ROAD

B2190

GRANGE LANE

ALLAND

ANTERBURY ROAD WEST CANTERBURY ROAD WEST A253

Minster-Thanet Cemetery

STREET

SEMPLE CL

SOUTHALL

HOUSE DR

HILL

BURGESS CL

TELEGRAPH HILL INDUSTRIAL ESTATE

FAIRFIELD RD

GDNS

ORCHARD CL

GREENHILL CL

PROSPECT GDS

ROAD

GRE

BROCKMANS CL

EDGAR RD

KENTON GDS

ROSE GDNS

Minster

FOXBOROUGH

LANE

LAUNDRY

THE

Wayborough Farm

WAYBOROUGH WAY

LANES

NKTON

PROSPECT ROAD

AUGUSTINE

FREMANS

EGBERT RD

ROAD

P

TOTHILL

HIGH STREET

ROAD

TAYLOR RD

THORNE RD

MOLINEUX

NORTON DR

ST MARYS RD

DOM CL

NEVA RD

SINGLETON CL

COURT

BEDLAM

DURLOCK

School

P C

RD

ST MILDREDS RD

Rec Grd

Abbey (remains)

Liby

CHURCH ST

CONYING HAM RD

ABBEY GRO

Watchester Farm

PETTS CRES

GLEBE CT

WATCHESTER LANE

STATION RD

STREET

MARSH FARM RD

STA APP

CHEESMANS CL

MINSTER

Greenham Bay

CLIFF ROAD

MINNIS BAY

Paddling Pool

PARADE
HEREWARD
SEA VIEW AV
SEA VIEW ROAD
GRENVILLE GDNS
GRENHAM
ANNA PARK
BERKELEY
HERSCHELL RD
DALL
INGER
SPENC
BORO
AY

THE ALFRED
HAROLD
ROAD
ETHELBERT
EGBERT RD
ROAD
GREEN
GATE
SEMAPHORE
HUNTING
HUNTINGTON
DARWIN
TYELL RD
BEACH
RD
SHAKES
ROAD
RD
GAINS
SPENC

THE PARADE
CP
WALKS
MINNIS
GRENHAM
RECULVER
ST MILDREDS
GALLWEY AV
NELSON
CUNNINGHAM
CRES
DUNCAN DR
MINNIS
GATE
MERCY
CY
ROSSETTI RD
STA
APP

MINNIS BAY

THE HENGIST
KINGS
QUEENS
CANUTE
AVENUE
DANE
HORSA RD
ARTHUR
ALFRED
ROAD
ROAD
FIRS
ROAD
GRENHAM
ROAD
CON
WAY
CUNNINGHAM
HUYTING
BIRCHINGTON
SANDLES
Li

Wantsum Walk   CP

DARYNGTON AV

DANE   ROAD

INGOLDSBY
ROAD
Gore End Farm
MINNIS
END
GORE
END
ROAD

Birchington

GORDON SQ
KEN
GDNS
SUSSEX
GDNS
SUPRE
GDNS
PROSPECT
RUTLAND
LINCOLN
GDNS
DORSET
GDNS
HERE
GDNS
OX

DEVON
ESSEX
LANCASTER
MANOR
GARDENS

MILL LA
ROW
MILL ROW
CANTERB
QUEX
ROSS
ED

KING
NOTTINGH
RD
SHERWOOD
RD
BROADLEY AV

4

5

Great Brooksend Farm

Brooks End

Upper Hale

Little Brooksend Farm

College Farm

6

CANTERBURY ROAD
SEAMARK ROAD
CRISPE
ROAD

A28
CANTERBURY

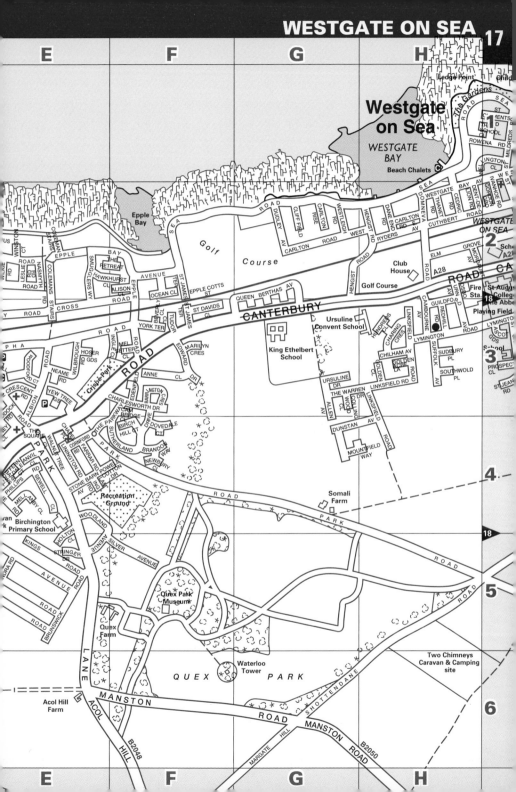

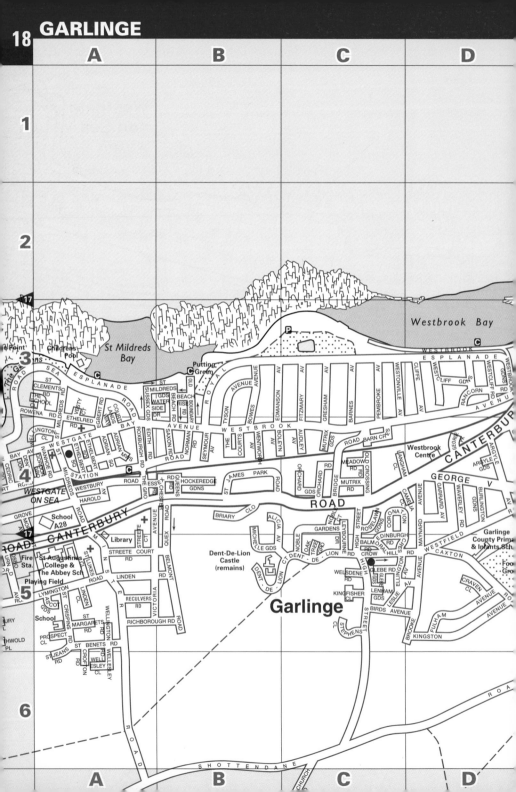

A   B   C   D

1

2

3

Westbrook Bay

St Mildreds Bay

WESTBROOK

ESPLANADE

Putting Green

Westbrook Centre

CANTERBURY

4

WESTGATE ON SEA

GEORGE V

Garlinge County Prima & Infants Sch

5

Fire Sta. St Augustines College & The Abbey Sch

Playing Field

School A28

Library

Dent-De-Lion Castle (remains)

Garlinge

6

SHOTTENDANE

A   B   C   D

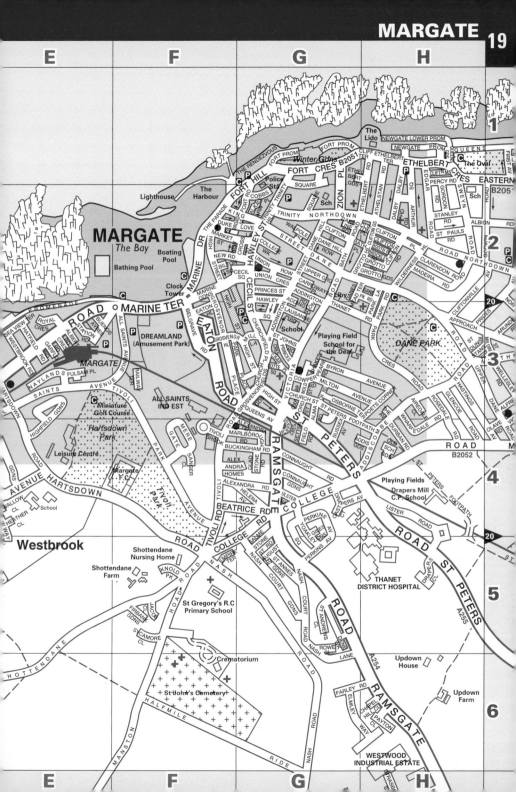

E F G H

1

ORENESS POINT

2

Botany
Bay

WALK
RIDINGS

BUCKHOLT
SPELDS
LARBET
LOWY
HURST
WAY

HALSTEAD
GDNS

EASTCHURCH

EYNS
FORD
CL

PENS
HURST
GDNS

COPPERHURST
WYE

SANDHURST

BUCK
HURST
DR

TEYNHAM
CL

OAKHAM
CHAL
CL

FORENESS
ROAD
ROAD

MARINE
DRIVE

DOLPHIN
COLETTE CL
AVENUE

SECOND
AV

DRIVE

AVENUE

C
Whiteness

Kingsgate
Bay

3

Captain Digby
Inn

ROAD
KINGSGATE
BAY RD

HOLLAND RD

Kingsgate
Castle

Hackemdown Point

FIRST
AV

FITZROY
AV CL

FITZROY

CAPEL

WOOD
LAND

OAKRIDGE

Kingsgate

ROAD

GAP
ROAD

JOSS

Joss Bay

4

PERCY

KINGSGATE

WHITENESS

C

WHITENESS

Golf Course

CONVENT

ROAD

C P

HILL
ROAD

BOTANY

GEORGE
HILL
ROAD

North Foreland
Golf Course

AVENUE

NTH FORELAND

5

ROSETOWER

LERRYN
GDNS

Club House

Kingsgate College

Reading Street

CONVENT

CRESCENT
RD

NORTH FORELAND

AVENUE

PROMENADE

Convalescent
Home

ASTOR

READING

ELMWOOD
STREET

North Foreland
Lighthouse

ROAD

GRAFTON

AFGHAN
RD

BALLIOL
RD

CHURCHFIELDS

TRIN
ITY
SQ

ELMWOOD
CL

ELMWOOD
GDNS

ELMWOOD

STREET

Elmwood
Farm

College

NORTH FORELAND
ROAD
B2052

NORTH
FORELAND
AVENUE

ANNES
RD

CLIFF

Nore
Point

6

MOCKETT
DR

LINK
RD

GREEN
RD

CEDAR
CL

THE
OAKS

THE
PADDOCKS

NORTHCLIFFE
GDNS

Convalescent
Home

CORONATION

ROAD

OLD
RD

School

FIG TREE RD

LANTHORN

GUY CL

KING
FRANCIS

CLIFF

ROAD

PROMENADE

▼
23

E F G H

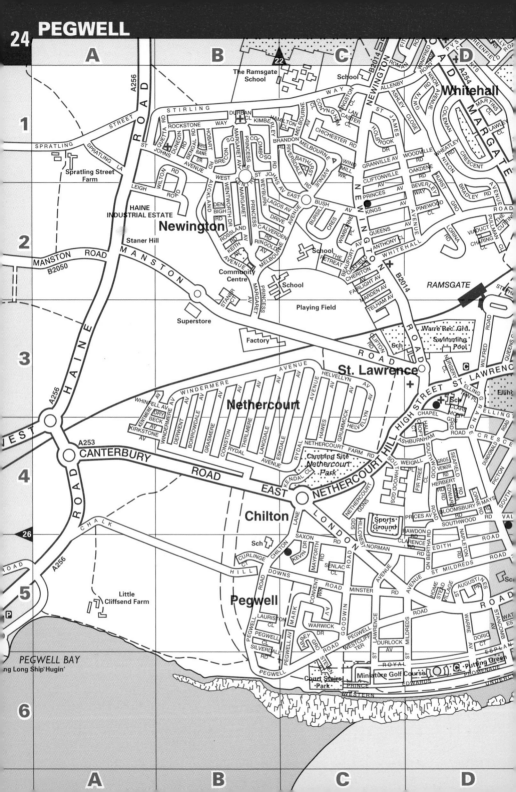

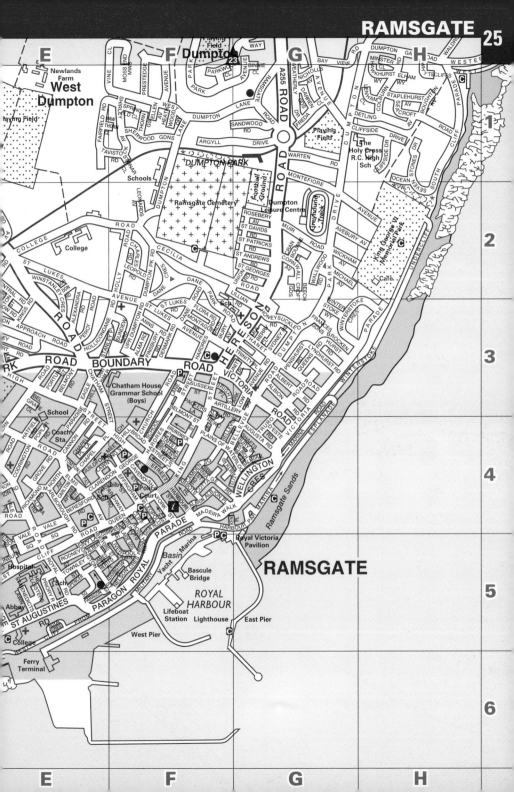

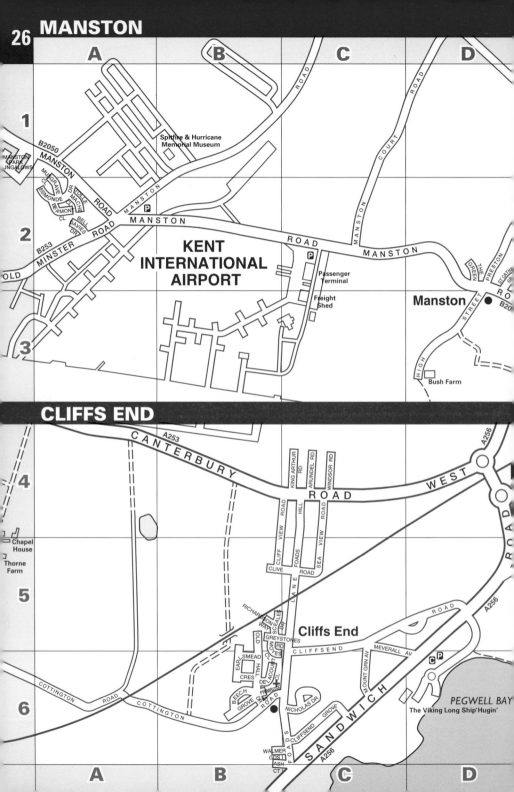

A   B   C   D

1

Spitfire & Hurricane
Memorial Museum

B2050

MANSTON

MANSTON PARK BUNGALOWS

MULGRAVE DR
ESMONDE
BEAUMON CL
TONE
MACHE PL
BELL
DAVIES DR

ROAD

MANSTON

P

2

B253
OLD
MINSTER ROAD

MANSTON

MANSTON ROAD

MANSTON

COURT ROAD

ROAD

KENT
INTERNATIONAL
AIRPORT

P

Passenger
Terminal

Freight
Shed

Manston ●

THE GREEN
PRESTON
ST CATH GR
HIGH STREET
B20

3

Bush Farm

CLIFFS END

A253

CANTERBURY

ROAD

WEST

A256

4

KING ARTHUR RD
ARUNDEL RD
WINDSOR RD

ROAD

Chapel
House

Thorne
Farm

CLIFF VIEW ROAD
FOADS HILL
SEA VIEW ROAD
CLIVE
ROAD
LANE

ROAD

A256

5

RICHARDSON RD
FONTAINE
WAT
OLD
HA
DE
GREYSTONES
RD
CRES
JACQUEL CL

Cliffs End

CLIFFSEND

MEVERALL AV

C P

EARL
SMEAD
HALL CRES
BEECH GROVE
PRIMROSE
ROAD

NICHOLAS DR

CLIFFSEND
FOADS ROAD
GROVE

MOUNT GRN AV

SANDWICH

PEGWELL BAY
The Viking Long Ship 'Hugin'

6

COTTINGTON ROAD

COTTINGTON

WALMER
GDSL
ASH
CT

A256

A   B   C   D

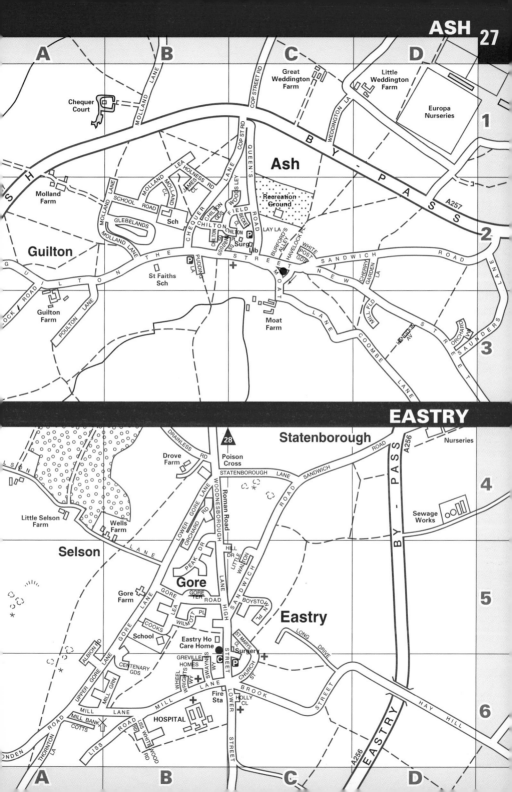

A   B   C   D

1

A257

White Mill Folk Museum

North Poulders

IND EST

THE CAUSEWAY   A S H   R O A D

Each End

Each End House

South Poulders

Sandwic

2

Marshborough Farm

Chestnut Farm

Marshborough

Vine Farm

SANDWICH

3

Parsonage Farm

White Cliffs Country Trail

POULDERS GDNS

SUNNYSIDE GS

WOODNESBOROUGH

Poulders Gardens

MARSHBOROUGH ROAD

MELVILLE LEA

STREET

SANDWICH ROAD WOODNESBOROUGH ROAD

4

BEACON LANE

OAK HILL

WOODLAND WY

THE

FOX TREE HILL

B Y - P A S S

JOHNS

Grove Manor Farm

CHURCH STREET

FOXBOROUGH

ST MARYS CL

Woodnesborough

Buckland Farm

5

SANDWICH ROAD

DRAINLESS ROAD

Hill Cross Farm

HILL

Highborough Hill

A256

SANDWICH

FELDERLAND

Fel F

6

A   B   C   D

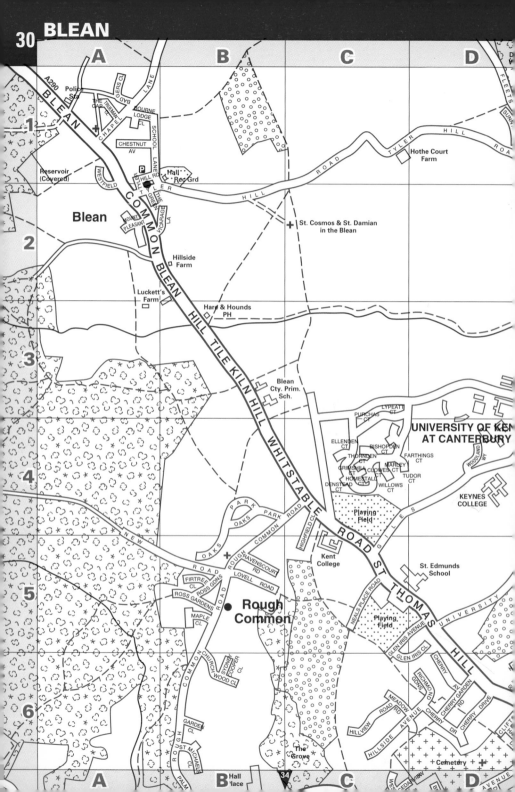

A290

BLEAN

Police Sta

THE TRUMAN
GAP

BADGERS CL

BOURNE
LODGE
CL

CHESTNUT
AV

CHAPEL

WESTFIELD

SCHOOL LANE

THE GREEN

P

TILE

HILL RD

Hall
Rec Grd

MOUNT
PLEASANT

Blean

VICARAGE
LA

Hillside
Farm

Luckett's
Farm

Hare & Hounds
PH

Reservoir
(Covered)

HILL

ROAD

TYLER

Hothe Court
Farm

HILL

FLEETS

SUNNY

HILL

RO

St. Cosmos & St. Damian
in the Blean

COMMON BLEAN

HILL TILE KILN HILL

WHITSTABLE

Blean Cty. Prim.
Sch.

LYPEATT
CT

PURCHAS
CT

ELLENDEN
CT

BISHOPDEN
CT

THORNDEN
CT

FARTHINGS
CT

GRIMSHILL
CT

CLOWES
CT

MARLEY
CT

HOMESTALL
CT

TUDOR
CT

DENSTEAD
CT

WILLOWS
CT

**UNIVERSITY OF KENT
AT CANTERBURY**

WOODLAND WY

KEYNES
COLLEGE

PARK

OAKS

PARK ROAD

COMMON ROAD

HIGHFIELD CL

ROAD

ST THOMAS

GILES

Playing
Field

NEW

OAKS

ROAD

RAVENSCOURT
RD

LOVELL ROAD

FIRTREE
CL

ROSS GDNS

ROSS GARDENS

MAPLE
CL

Kent
College

St. Edmunds
School

NEALS PLACE ROAD

UNIVERSITY

HILL

Playing
Field

**Rough
Common**

CHURCH

COMMON

SYDNEY
COOPER

WOOD CL

ROAD

GARDEN
CL

ST MICHAELS

PALM

GLEN IRIS AVENUE

GLEN IRIS CL

CHERRY

AV

RICHMOND

GDNS

CHERRY

AVENUE

CHERRY GARDEN

RD

CHERRY

DR

CHERRY DRIVE

MEADOW
ROAD

HILLVIEW

HILLSIDE

AVENUE

CEDAR WAY

The Grove

Cemetery

WEST

CLIFTON

AVENUE

Hall
Place

34

E **F** **G** **H**

Honey Wood

Great Hall Wood

1

Barton Wood

HACKINGTON ROAD

SUMMER LANE

PARK FARM CL

WOOD HILL

Tyler Hill

Little Hall Wood

2

Brickhouse Wood

CANTERBURY HILL

32

ST STEPHENS ROAD

LANE

3

DARWIN COLLEGE

Library

benkian theatre

RUTHERFORD COLLEGE

ELIOT COLLEGE

The Archbishop's C.E. Sec. Sch.

HACKINGTON DOWNS

Hales Place

LONG MEADOW WAY

THE CLOSE

THE CROSS WAYS

TENTERDEN

GREEN DELL

PLAINE

HAWE

BAWDEN CLOSE

COPINGER

WAY

NETHERSOLE

BRUNTON GDNS

HEADCORN GDNS

BROADHURST

KILNDOWN

WESTERHAM

LEONIAN

BICKLEY

KEMSING

TUNSTALL

ANDRESS

CULPEPPER

HOVENDEN

FRENCHAM

DILNOT

KEMSING

GODDEN

MON FORT CL

JESUIT

LONG

HEADCORN DRIVE

KEMSING

ULCOMBE

4

THE CRESCENT

ORCHARD

MANWOOD

THE

THE AV

MOORFIELD

THE TERRACE

WICHLING CL

DRIVE

PENSHURST

FARLEIGH

HEVER

OAK ROAD

BROAD ROAD

32

CI BUSI PA

HILL

TYLER CL

LYNDHURST CL

STEPHENSON RD

LEYCROFT CL

RINGWOOD CL

SMYTHE CL

Sch

ST STEPHENS GRN

St. Stephens School

Rec. Grd.

Playing Field

HALES DRIVE

ST STEPHENS

ORDNAM CL

FAVERSHAM RD

BLEAN

STANFORD RD

LICH

ST MICHAELS RD

BEACONSFIELD RD

WACHER CL

ST STEPHENS

ST STEPHENS RD

Superstores

Vauxhall Lakes

RIVERDALE

PARHAM RD

GLENSIDE

BRAMSHAW

SALISBURY ROAD

BIRCHWOOD WALK

REDWOOD

VERWOOD CL

PINE TREE AVENUE

St. Stephen's Playing Field

HACKINGTON TER

HANOVER RD

ABBEY GDNS

MONKS CL

HAWTHORN AV

WILLOW

Great Stour

OAK WAY

Kingsmead Stadium

ARRAN MS

GORE MS

GREEN CLOTH MS

MARY GRN WK

METCALFE MS

HONEYWOOD

BALCRAFT

MILL RD

BARTON RD

A28

BROMORE CL

HUDSON

TIDDING

REGENCY

5

6

PENHOUSE

PINE TREE AVENUE

LONGACRE

FORTY ACRES RD

MANDEVILLE RD

BEVERLEY RD

ROSEACRE

COPER GATE

ROPER RD

SHEPHERD GATE

STATION RD

Playing Field

Playing Field

ST STEPHENS CL

MALTHOUSE RD

ST STEPHENS ROAD

KINGSMEAD ROAD

BROAD OAK ROAD

Leisure Centre

Playing Field

Supermarket

Sch

CATHEDRAL VIEW

Kingsmead Stadium

NEW TOWN

COLD HARBOUR

A28

STABLE RD

35

TOURTEL ROAD

Council Offices

E **WEST** **F** **G** **H**

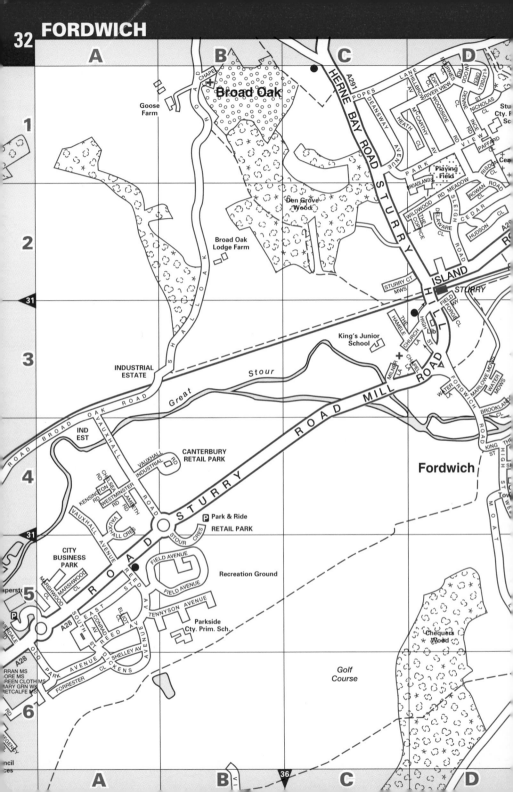

FORDWICH

Broad Oak

Goose Farm

Den Grove Wood

Broad Oak Lodge Farm

HERNE BAY ROAD

A291

POPES

DEANSWAY

HEATH AV

PARK AVENUE

STURRY

ISLAND

STURRY

Playing Field

ROADLANDS

MEADOW RD

SLEIGH ROAD

CEDAR

HUDSON

NICHOLAS

PAFFORD

ROWAN ROAD

RISDON

DELAWARE CL

THE COPPICE

STURRY CT MWS

King's Junior School

INDUSTRIAL ESTATE

Stour

Great

Stour

ROAD

BROAD OAK ROAD

IND EST

VAUXHALL

CANTERBURY RETAIL PARK

VAUXHALL INDUSTRIAL

KENSINGTON RD

CHELTON RD

WESTMINSTER RD

LAMBETH RD

VAUXHALL CRES

STURRY

ROAD

MILL ROAD

Fordwich

THE HAMELE

CHURCH LA

MILLER'S FIELD

CHAPEL

WATER

FORDWICH

MARLOWE MDWS

WATER MDWS

BROOKLANDS CL

KING ST

HIGH ST

Park & Ride
RETAIL PARK

CITY BUSINESS PARK

VAUXHALL AVENUE

VAUXHALL CRES

STOUR CRES

FIELD AVENUE

FIELD AVENUE

Recreation Ground

A28

MARSHWOOD CL

MARSHWOOD CL

REED AV

SOUTH ST

EAST AV

CONRAD AV

ELIOT

REED AV

TENNYSON AVENUE

SHELLEY AV

DICKENS

Parkside Cty. Prim. Sch.

FORRESTER

A28

Golf Course

Chequers Wood

RRAN MS
ORE MS
REEN CLOTH MS
MARY GRN WY
ETCALFE MS

REGENCY

ncil
ces

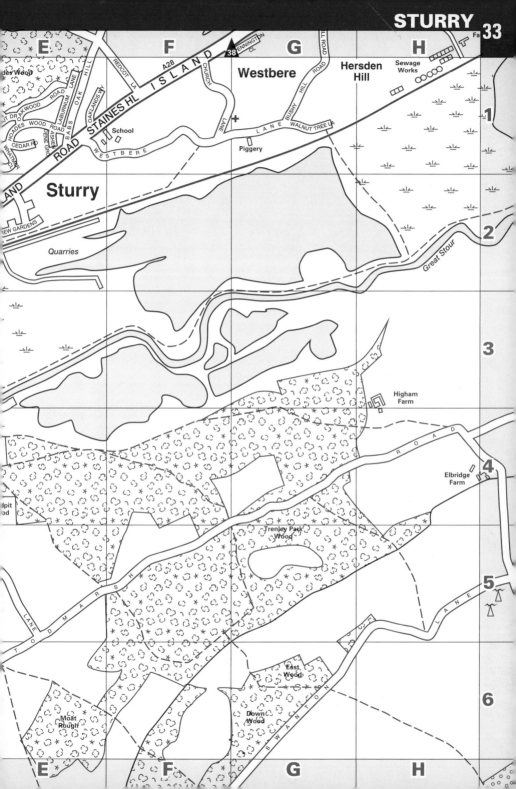

E F G H Fa

Westbere

Hersden Hill

Sewage Works

des Wood

A28

School

Sturry

Piggery

IEW GARDENS

Quarries

Great Stour

1

2

3

Higham Farm

lpit od

Trenley Park Wood

Elbridge Farm

4

5

East Wood

6

Moat Rough

Down Wood

E F G H

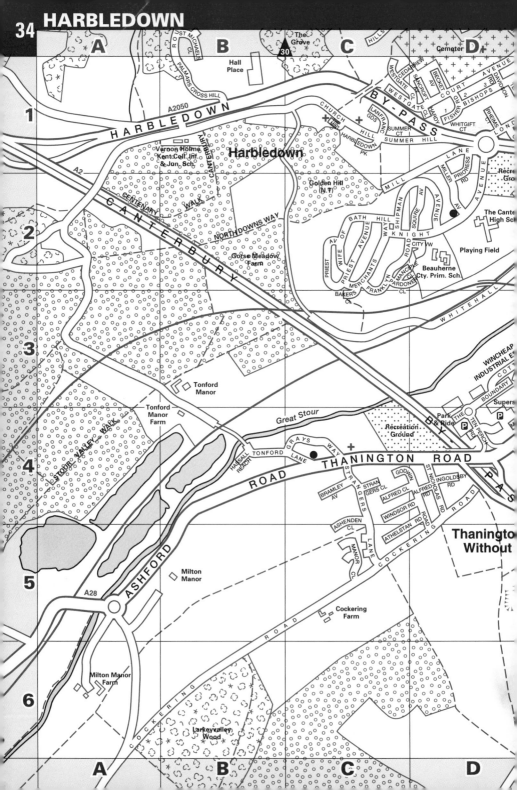

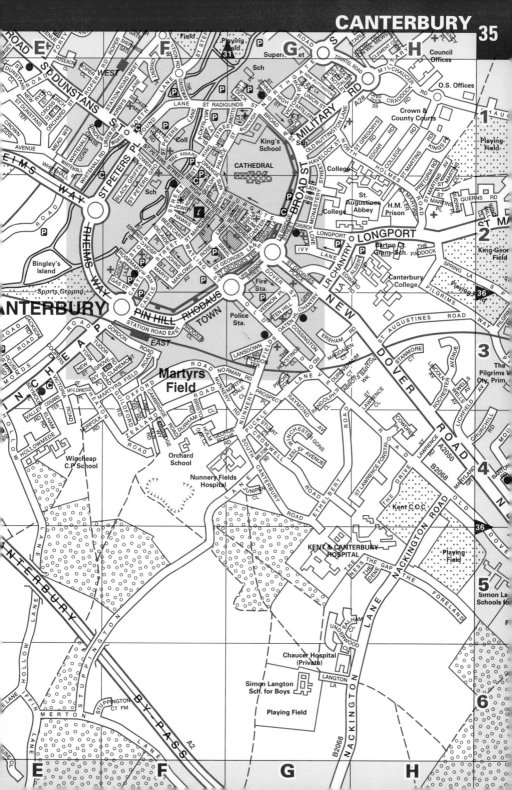

A   B ▲32   C   D

S. Offices

CHAUCER

1

Playing Field

SOBRAON WY
PILCKEM
TUNIS
YPRES
SANGRO
DOURO
SOMME
ALBURT
CAMBRAI
BLENHEIM AV
SEVASTOPOL
PL
PL

VILLIERS ROAD

Scotland Hills

Christ Church College
Post Graduate Centre

TALAVERA
ROAD
WEMYSS
BOTHEGA
RD

Howe Barracks

STODMARSH

ST MARTINS HILL LITTLEBOURNE ROAD
A257

2

St MARTINS

ST. MARTINS HOSPITAL

King George's Field

WARWICK
SOMERSET
RD
AVON CL
ROAD
WINNMA RD

KENT DEVON RD
NONSUCH
STRME
RD
LAXTON WY
SUFFOLK RD
ESSEX RD
RUTLAND
CL
DORSET
RD
HAMPSHIRE
RD
SURREY
RD
CUMBERLAND
CORNWALL GDNS
SUSSEX
AVENUE

BEKESBOURNE

SPRING LA

Play
35 field

RIMS
ROAD

PILGRIMS WAY
RUSSELL CL
WINSTON CL
SPRING
CL

Hoath Farm

WINCHESTER

3

CHESTER AVENUE
SWELLS AV
LICHFIELD

The Pilgrims Way
Cty. Prim. Sch.

Chaucer Tech. Coll.

PYRCH
GRIMS
DRYMEN
CHAUCER CL
ROAD

Little Barton Farm

Playing Field

WAY

DOWNS

Palmsted Wood

ROAD
A2050
N68

4

CHURCHILL
MOUNT
BARTON ROAD
BARTON
MILTON CL
COBHAM
CL

NEW

ROAD
A2050
DOVER

MARY CRT
OLD

5

35

Playing Field

Simon Langton Schools for Girls

Playing Field

School

Haystack Wood

IRELAND

DOVER ROAD

Hode Farm

6

Milestone

A   B   C ▼37   D

A · B · C · D

36

Haystack
Wood

BEKESBOURNE LANE · OAKLEIGH LANE

BEKESBOURNE

BEKESBOURNE LANE

1

Hode
Farm

BEKESBOURNE

HILL

ROAD · SCHOOL LANE

2

BIFRONS HILL

BIFRONS
RD

STATION

Patrixbourne

THE STREET

ST MARYS RD

Bifrons
Gardens

Fords

Bifron's Park

ROAD

KEEPERS

3

A2

B R I D G E

Bourne

BEKESBOURNE
RD

Elham Valley Way

Nail

PATRIXBOURNE

HILL

4

ROAD

HIGH

CONYNGHAM

LANE

THE NEW

The
Close

**Bridge & Patrixbourne
C.E. Prim. Sch.**

Anglo-Saxon
Burial Ground

PETT

HILL

DERING CL

DERING RD

FILMER RD

SAXON
ROAD

**Police
Office**

Rec.
Grd.

RIVERSIDE RD

PATRIXBOURNE ROAD

UNION

THE
CLOSE

CHURCHILL

WESTERN AV

WINDMILL

GREEN

RIVER
SIDE M

STREET

5

TER
VIEW

BOURNE

WINDMILL
LANE

FORD

BRIDGEFORD
WAY

BREWERY LA

MEADOW
CL

Bridge

B Y · P A S S

Brickfield
Farm

Ford

BOURNE PARK ROAD

RIDGE

BEECH HILL

BRIDGE DOWN

Cricket
Ground

Highland Court
Annexe
(Kent & Canterbury
Hospital)

BOURNE PARK ROAD

Tumuli

BRIDGE DOWN

HIGHAM

PIPPN RD

A2

Cold Stores

6

Warren
Plantation

A · B · C · D

A **B** **C** **D**

1 **2** **3**

Ickham

Reynolds Place

White Bridge

Treasury Farm

Littlebourne Court

Ickh Ha

Littlebourne C.E. Prim. Sch.

Nev F

Rec. Grd.

TREASURY VW

Littlebourne

Little Stour

HIGH STREET

THE HILL

ST. VINCENTS CL
THE ELDERS
COURT MEADOWS
PINESIDE RD
HILLCREST RD
EVENHILL RD
NEWING CL
JUBILEE RD
ROSE ACRE RD
ORCHARD CL
THE MEALINGS
THE GREEN
NARGATE
HILL ROAD
CHURCH ROAD
ELMLEIGH RD
NARGATE STREET
BUILDERS SQ
NARGATE
DRILL STREET
WICKHAM LA
THE STREET
SCHOOL LANE
CHERVILLE LANE

COURT
BEKESBOURNE LANE
THE LANE

HERSDEN / WESTBERE

A **B** **C** **D**

4 **5** **6**

Joiners Farm

Gravel Pit

Hersden Cty. Prim. Sch.

Hersder

Bredlands Farm

Bredlands Farm

Hoplands Farm

Playing Field

Montgomery School

Haseden Farm

Sewage Works

Westbere

Hersden Hill

School

Piggery

33

A28

HOATH ROAD
BREDLANDS
ISLAND ROAD
ISLAND ROAD
PENNINGTON CL
BUSHY HILL ROAD
CHURCH LANE
BUSHY HILL LANE
WALNUT TREE LA
REDCO
NES HL
STBERE
THE LANE
ST ALBANS RD
SUTTON RD
AVENUE
THE OAKS
THE POPLARS
EAST VW
NORTH VW
ROA
ASH CRESCENT
THE ELMS
THE SYCAMORES
MAPLE CT
MAPLE GDNS

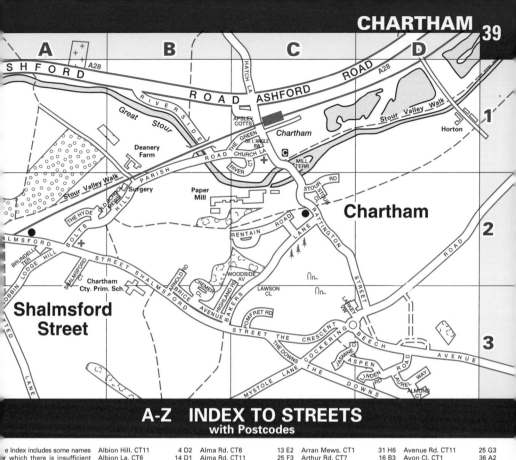

A-Z INDEX TO STREETS
with Postcodes

Clifton Rd. CT9 3 F2
Clifton Rd. CT5 9 E3
Clifton Rd. CT11 24 C3
Clifton St. CT9 3 E2
Cliftonville Av. CT9 20 A3
Cliftonville Av. CT12 24 C2
Cliftonville Mews. CT9 19 H1
Clive Rd. CT9 22 A3
Clive Rd. CT12 26 B5
Clovelly Rd. CT5 9 E5
Clover Rise. CT5 10 A4
Clowes Ct. CT2 30 C4
Clyde St. CT1 35 G1
Coastguard Alley. CT5 8 D2
Cobblers Bridge Rd. CT6 12 A3
Cobbs Pl. CT9 3 D2
Cobden Pl. CT1 6 C2
Cobham Cl. CT1 36 A4
Cockering Rd. CT1 34 C5
Cockering Rd. CT4 39 C3
Codrington Rd. CT11 4 A2
Cogans Ter. CT1 35 E3
Colburn Rd. CT10 25 H1
Cold Harbour. CT1 31 G6
Coleman Cres. CT12 24 D1
Coleman Stairs. CT7 17 E2
Colemans Stairs Rd. CT7 17 E2
Colemans Yard. CT11 4 C2
Colette Cl. CT10 21 F3
Colewood Rd. CT5 10 D3
Collard Cl. CT6 12 D3
College Rd. CT9 19 G4
College Rd. CT11 25 E2
College Rd. CT1 35 H1
College Wk. CT9 19 G2
Collingwood Cl. CT8 17 G3
Collingwood Cl. CT10 23 E4
Collingwood Rd. CT5 9 E3
Collins Rd. CT6 11 H4
Colombo Sq. CT12 24 B1
Columbia Av. CT5 8 C5
Columbus Av. CT12 15 C2
*Conference Wk, Russett Rd. CT1 36 A2
*Conifer Ct, Adrian Sq. CT9 18 A4
Coniston Av. CT11 24 B4
Connaught Gdns. CT9 19 G4
Connaught Rd. CT9 19 G4
Conrad Av. CT1 32 A5
Constable Rd. CT7 16 D2
Consul Cl. CT6 11 F2
Continental App. CT9 22 A2
Convent Rd. CT10 21 F4
Convent Walk. CT11 24 C5
Conway Cl. CT7 16 C3
Conyngham Cl. CT12 24 C1
Conyngham La. CT4 37 B4
Conyngham Rd. CT6 13 F1
Conyngham Rd. CT12 15 B6
Cooks Lea. CT13 27 B5
Coombe La. CT3 27 D3
Coombe Walk. CT5 7 A4
*Coopers Hill, Charles St. CT6 12 C1
Coopers La. CT1 35 E3
Cop St Rd. CT3 27 C1
Copinger Cl. CT2 31 G4
Copper Gate. CT2 31 F6
Copperfield Ct. CT10 5 D3
Copperhurst Walk. CT9 21 E3
Copt Cl. CT2 32 D1
Cornford Rd. CT7 17 E4
Cornhill. CT11 4 C3
Cornwall Av. CT11 25 G2
Cornwall Gdns. CT9 20 B3
Cornwall Gdns. CT1 36 A3
Cornwall Rd. CT6 11 G4
Cornwallis Av. CT6 13 E3
Cornwallis Circle. CT5 9 E3
Cornwallis Gdns. CT10 23 G2
Coronation Cl. CT10 21 E6
Coronation Cres. CT9 18 C4
Coronation Rd. CT11 4 A2
*Corsican Walk, Cornwallis Av. CT6 13 F3
Corylus Dr. CT5 8 C5
Cossington Rd. CT1 6 D5
Cottage Rd. CT11 4 D2
Cottage Row. CT13 29 E1
Cottington Rd. CT12 26 A6
Cotton Rd. CT1 34 D3
Coulter Rd. CT6 11 G4
Court Hill. CT3 38 A1
Court Mdws. CT3 38 A2
Court Rd. CT7 14 A5
Courtlands. CT6 12 D3
Courtlands Way. CT8 18 A3
Coventon La. CT14 29 F5
Coventry Gdns. CT6 13 G1
Cow La. CT1 34 D3
Cowdrey Pl. CT1 35 H4
Cowley Rise. CT9 20 B6
Cowper Cl. CT5 10 C3
Cowper Rd. CT9 3 E4
Coxes Av. CT12 22 B5
Coxes La. CT12 22 B5
Craddock Dr. CT1 35 H1
Craddock Rd. CT1 35 H1
Crampton Ct. CT10 5 A3
*Cranborne Wk, Salisbury Rd. CT2 31 E5
Cranbourne Cl. CT11 25 G2
Cranbrook Cl. CT9 21 E4
Cranleigh Gdns. CT5 9 F4
Craven Cl. CT9 18 D5
Crawford Gdns. CT9 20 A3
Crawford Rd. CT10 23 F3
Cremer Cl. CT4 39 B2
Crescent Rd. CT9 3 A3
Crescent Rd. CT7 17 E3
Crescent Rd. CT10 21 G5
Crescent Rd. CT11 24 D4
Cresta Cl. CT6 11 E2
Crispe Rd. CT7 16 C6
Crofton Rd. CT8 18 A5
Crofts Pl. CT10 5 C3
Cromwell Rd. CT5 9 E3
Cromwell Rd. CT1 35 G4
Cross Rd. CT7 17 E3
Cross St. CT6 12 A3
Cross St. CT2 35 E1
Crossley Av. CT6 11 E2
Crossways. CT2 31 F4
Crossways Av. CT9 22 A3
Crow Hill. CT10 5 B1
Crow Hill Rd. CT9 18 C5
Crown Gdns. CT2 35 E1
Crown Hill Rd. CT6 11 G2
Crundale Way. CT9 21 E4
Crystal Business Centre. CT13 29 G1
Cudham Gdns. CT9 20 D3
Culpepper Cl. CT2 31 G4
Cumberland Av. CT10 5 B1
Cumberland Av. CT1 36 B3
Cumberland Rd. CT11 4 A2
Cumberland Rd. CT9 20 A3
Cundishall Cl. CT5 8 D4
Cunningham Cres. CT7 16 C3
Curlew Cl. CT6 13 E4
Curlinge Ct. CT11 24 B5
Curtis Wood Park Rd. CT6 14 C2
Curtis Wood Rd. CT6 14 C2
Cushman Rd. CT1 35 E3
Cuthbert Rd. CT8 17 H2
Cypress Cl. CT5 8 D5

D'Este Rd. CT11 4 F1
Daimler Av. CT6 11 F2
Dalby Rd. CT9 3 F2
Dalby Sq. CT9 3 F1
Dallinger Rd. CT7 16 C3
Dalmaney Cl. CT10 5 C2
Dalmeny Av. CT9 20 C4
Damerham Cl. CT2 31 E5
Dane Court Gdns. CT10 22 D2
Dane Court Rd. CT10 22 C1
Dane Cres. CT11 25 F2
Dane End Rd. CT8 17 H2
Dane Gdns. CT9 20 B6
Dane Hill. CT9 3 E2
Dane Hill Gro. CT9 3 E2
Dane Hill Row. CT9 3 E2
Dane Mt. CT9 20 B6
Dane Park Rd. CT9 3 F3
Dane Park Rd. CT11 25 F2
Dane Rd. CT9 3 E2
Dane Rd. CT7 16 A3
Dane Rd. CT11 25 F3
Dane Valley Rd. CT9 20 A5
Danesmead Ter. CT9 3 F3
Daniels Ct. CT5 8 D3
Darenth Cl. CT6 12 D4
Dargate Rd. CT5 7 A4
Darnley Cl. CT10 23 F5
Darrell Cl. CT6 11 H3
Darren Gdns. CT10 23 F6
Darwin Rd. CT7 16 D3
Daryngton Av. CT7 16 A3
David Av. CT9 20 C3
Davids Cl. CT10 5 C5
Davidson Rd. CT2 34 D1
Daytona Way. CT6 11 E2
De L'Angle Row. CT4 39 C1
Deal Rd. CT14 29 E5
Deal Rd. CT13 29 E5
Dean Croft. CT6 13 E5
Deane Cl. CT5 9 F5
Deansway Av. CT2 32 C1
Deborah Cl. CT5 9 G5
Delacourt Cl. CT12 26 B6
Delaware Cl. CT2 32 D2
Delf St. CT13 29 E1
Delfside. CT13 29 F3
Delmar Cl. CT5 10 C3
Denbigh Rd. CT12 24 B2
Dence Cl. CT6 12 D2
Dence Park. CT6 12 D2
Dene Wk. CT9 19 G5
Denmark Rd. CT11 25 F3
Denne Cl. CT2 32 D1
Denstead Ct. CT2 30 C4
Dent-de-Lion Ct. CT9 18 B5
Dent-de-Lion Rd. CT8 17 H2
Dent-de-Lion Rd. CT9 18 C5
Denton Way. CT9 20 B4
Dering Cl. CT4 37 B4
Dering Rd. CT6 12 B2
Dering Rd. CT4 37 B4
Derwent Av. CT11 24 B4
Detling Av. CT10 25 G1
*Devon Ct, Stirling Way. CT12 24 C1
Devon Gdns. CT7 16 D4
Devon Rd. CT1 36 A2
Devonshire Gdns. CT9 20 B3
Devonshire Ter. CT10 5 C3
Diamond Rd. CT5 9 F2
Dickens Av. CT1 32 A6
Dickens Rd. CT10 5 C2
Dickens Walk. CT10 5 C3
*Discovery Wk, Russet Rd. CT1 36 A2
Doggerel Acre. CT5 9 G5
Dolphin Cl. CT10 21 F3
Dolphin St. CT6 12 B1
Domneva Rd. CT12 15 B5
Domneva Rd. CT8 17 H2
Donegal Rd. CT1 36 A2
Donnahay Rd. CT12 22 C5
Dorcas Gdns. CT10 23 G2
Doric Ct. CT11 24 D5
Dorothy Dr. CT12 22 C6
Dorset Cl. CT5 8 C5
*Dorset Ct, Stirling Way. CT12 24 C1
Dorset Gdns. CT7 16 D4
Dorset Rd. CT1 36 B3
Douglas Av. CT5 9 F3
Douglas Cl. CT10 23 E3
Douglas Rd. CT6 12 C3
Douro Cl. CT1 36 B1
Dove Cl. CT5 8 D5
Dovedale. CT7 17 F4
Dovedale Ct. CT7 17 F4
Dover Rd. CT13 29 F3
Dover St. CT1 6 D4
Down Barton Rd. CT7 14 A6
Downs Av. CT5 9 F3
Downs Pk. CT6 12 D2
Downs Rd. CT11 24 B5
Downs Rd. CT2 31 F4
Drainless Rd. CT13 27 B4
Drapers Av. CT9 19 G4
Drapers Cl. CT9 19 H5
Drill La. CT3 38 C1
Drybeck Av. CT11 24 A3
Dryden Cl. CT1 36 A3
Duck La. CT1 6 C2
Dudley Av. CT8 17 G2
Duke St. CT9 3 D2
Dumpton Gap Rd. CT10 23 G6
Dumpton La. CT11 25 F2
Dumpton Park Dr. CT11 25 G3
Dumpton Park Rd. CT11 25 F2
Duncan Dr. CT7 16 C3
Duncan Rd. CT11 4 A2
Duncan Rd. CT5 9 E4
Dundonald Rd. CT10 5 C4
Dundonald Rd. CT11 24 D4
Dunedin Rd. CT12 24 B1
*Dunoon Ct, Argyll Dr. CT11 25 G1
Dunstan Av. CT8 17 G4
Durban Cl. CT12 24 B1
Durban Rd. CT9 19 H4
Durham Cl. CT1 35 F4
Durlock. CT12 15 C6
Durlock Av. CT11 24 C5
Durlock Rd. CT3 27 A3
Durnford Cl. CT2 31 E5
Durovernum Ct. CT1 35 G3

Eagle Hill. CT11 25 E3
Ealham Cl. CT4 35 G5
Earlsmead Cres. CT12 26 B6
East Cliff Par. CT6 12 D1
East Cliff Prom. CT10 23 H2
East Northdown Cl. CT9 21 E4
East St. CT6 12 C1
East St. CT1 32 A5
East Vw. CT3 38 D4
Eastchurch Rd. CT9 20 D3
Eastern Esplanade. CT9 20 A2
Eastern Esplanade. CT10 23 H2
Eastfield Rd. CT7 17 E3
Eastgate Cl. CT6 12 D4
Eastry Cl. CT5 10 D3
Eaton Hill. CT9 3 C3
Eaton Rd. CT9 3 C3
Eddie Willet Rd. CT6 11 G3
Eddington Business Pk. CT6 12 B4
Eddington La. CT6 12 B4
Eddington Way. CT6 12 B4
Eden Rd. CT5 8 B5
Edenfield. CT7 17 F3
Edgar Cl. CT5 10 C3
Edgar Rd. CT12 15 A5
Edgar Rd. CT9 19 H1
Edgar Rd. CT1 35 H1
Edge End Rd. CT10 23 F4
Edinburgh Rd. CT9 18 C5
*Edinburgh Wk, Edinburgh Rd. CT9 18 C5
Edith Rd. CT8 18 A4
Edith Rd. CT11 24 D5
Edmanson Av. CT9 18 B4
Edward Dr. CT7 17 F3
Edward Rd. CT5 7 C1
Edward Rd. CT1 35 G2
Effingham St. CT11 4 C2
Egbert Rd. CT12 15 B5
Egbert Rd. CT7 16 B3
Egbert Rd. CT8 18 A4
Egerton Dr. CT9 20 D3
Elfrida Cl. CT9 20 C5
*Elham Cl, Tenterden Way. CT9 20 B4
Elham Rd. CT1 35 E4
Elham Way. CT10 23 G6
Elizabeth Ct. CT10 23 H1
Elizabeth Rd. CT11 4 E2
Elizabeth Way. CT6 12 D3
Ellen Av. CT11 25 F1
Ellenden Ct. CT2 30 C4
Ellington Av. CT9 18 C5
Ellington Pl. CT11 24 D3
Ellington Rd. CT11 24 D3
Elliot Cl. CT1 32 A5
Ellis Rd. CT5 10 A3
Ellis Way. CT6 13 E4
Ellison Cl. CT5 10 B5
*Ellison Cl, Russett Rd. CT1 36 A2
Elm Gro. CT8 17 H2
Elm Wood Cl. CT5 10 B4
Elm Wood West. CT5 10 B4
Elmleigh Rd. CT3 38 B2
Elmley Way. CT9 19 G6
Elms Av. CT11 4 B2
Elmstone Gdns. CT9 20 D4
Elmstone Rd. CT11 25 E3
Elmwood Av. CT10 21 F6
Elmwood Cl. CT10 21 F6
Emmerson Gdns. CT5 10 B3
Empire Ter. CT9 19 F5
Enterprise Rd. CT9 22 A2
Enticott Cl. CT5 9 H3
Epping Cl. CT6 12 D5
Epple Bay Av. CT7 17 E2
Epple Bay Rd. CT7 16 D3
Epple Cotts St. CT7 17 F2
Epple Rd. CT7 17 F2
Ersham Rd. CT1 35 G3
Eskdale Av. CT11 24 C4
Esmonde Dr. CT12 26 A2
Esplanade. CT8 18 A3
Essex Av. CT6 11 F2
Essex Gdns. CT7 16 D4
Essex Rd. CT8 18 A4
Essex Rd. CT1 36 B2
Essex St. CT5 9 E4
Ethel Rd. CT10 5 A2
Ethelbert Cres. CT9 19 H1
Ethelbert Gdns. CT9 3 F1
Ethelbert Rd. CT9 3 F2
Ethelbert Rd. CT11 4 B2
Ethelbert Rd. CT7 16 B2
Ethelbert Rd. CT1 35 G4
Ethelbert Sq. CT8 18 A4
Ethelbert Ter. CT9 3 F1
*Ethelbert Ter, Ethelbert Sq. CT8 18 A4
Ethelred Rd. CT8 18 A4
Evenhill Rd. CT3 38 A2
Eynsford Cl. CT9 21 E3

Fair St. CT10 23 E4
Fairacre. CT10 23 E4
Fairacres Cl. CT6 13 F3
Fairfax Dr. CT6 13 H1
Fairfield Pk. CT10 23 E4
Fairfield Rd. CT12 15 B4
Fairfield Rd. CT10 23 E4
Fairfield Rd. CT11 25 E1
Fairlawn. CT5 10 C5
Fairlawn Rd. CT12 22 B5
Fairlight Av. CT12 24 C2
Fairoaks. CT6 13 E3
Fairview Cl. CT9 3 F2
Fairview Gdns. CT2 33 E2
Fairway Cres. CT5 8 B5
Farleigh Rd. CT2 31 G4
Farley Rd. CT9 19 G6
Farm House Cl. CT5 9 G4
Farrar Rd. CT7 17 E4
Farthings Ct. CT2 30 C4
Faversham Rd. CT5 8 A5
Felderland Cl. CT14 29 E6
Felderland La. CT13 28 D6
Fenoulhet Way. CT6 12 C2
Fern Cl. CT5 10 B5
Fern Ct. CT10 5 C2
Ferndale Ct. CT7 17 E4
Fernlea Av. CT6 12 A3
Field Av. CT1 32 A5
Field View. CT5 8 C5
Field Way. CT2 32 D3
*Fiesta Wk, Russett Rd. CT1 36 A2
Fife Rd. CT6 11 G3
Fifth Av. CT9 20 B2
Fig Tree Rd. CT10 23 F1
Filmer Rd. CT4 37 B5
Finsbury Rd. CT11 25 F3
Fir Tree Cl. CT11 24 D4
Fir Tree Hill. CT13 28 A5
Firbank Gdns. CT9 19 F5
Firbanks. CT5 9 H4
First Av. CT9 20 A2
First Av. CT10 21 E3
Firtree Cl. CT2 30 B5
Fisher Rd. CT2 34 D1
Fisher St. CT13 29 F2
Fitzgerald Av. CT6 11 H2
Fitzmary Av. CT9 18 C4
Fitzroy Av. CT9 20 A4
Fitzroy Av. CT10 21 F4
Fitzroy Av. CT12 22 B6
Fitzroy Rd. CT5 9 H1
Fleets La. CT2 30 D1
Fleetwood Av. CT6 12 A3
Fletcher Rd. CT5 10 A4
Flora Rd. CT11 25 F3
Florence Av. CT5 8 C5
Florence Rd. CT11 4 A3
Foads Hill. CT12 26 C5
Foads La. CT12 26 C6
Ford Cl. CT6 11 F2
Ford Cl. CT4 37 B5
Ford Hill. CT6 13 H6
Ford Walk. CT5 7 A4
Fordoun Rd. CT10 5 A3
Fordwich Gro. CT10 20 D6
Fordwich Pl. CT13 29 E3
Fordwich Rd. CT2 32 D3
Foreland Av. CT9 20 C3
Foreness Cl. CT10 21 F2
Forge Cl. CT2 32 D3
Forge La. CT5 9 E4
Forgefields. CT6 14 D1
Forrester Cl. CT1 32 A6
Fort Aragon. CT9 3 E1

Fort Cres. CT9 — 3 D1
Fort Hill. CT9 — 3 D1
Fort Lower Prom. CT9 — 3 E1
Fort Prom. CT9 — 3 E1
Fort Rd. CT9 — 3 D2
Fort Rd. CT10 — 5 D3
Fortuna Ct. CT11 — 25 E3
Forty Acres Rd. CT2 — 31 E6
Fosters Av. CT10 — 20 D6
*Fountain St,
  Harbour St. CT5 — 9 E1
Fox Dene Rd. CT5 — 8 B5
Foxborough Cl. CT13 — 28 A5
Foxborough Hill. CT13 — 28 A4
Foxborough La. CT12 — 15 B5
Foxdown Cl. CT2 — 31 E6
Foxgrove Rd. CT5 — 9 H2
Foxs Cross Hill. CT5 — 7 A3
Foxs Cross Rd. CT5 — 7 B3
Frances Gdns. CT11 — 25 G3
Francis Rd. CT10 — 23 G1
Franklyn Rd. CT2 — 34 C2
Freda Cl. CT10 — 25 G1
Freemans Cl. CT5 — 8 B6
Freemans Rd. CT12 — 15 B5
Frencham Cl. CT2 — 31 G4
Freshlands. CT6 — 13 G1
Freshwater Cl. CT6 — 11 G3
Friars Cl. CT5 — 9 G2
Friary Way. CT2 — 30 D6
Friendly Cl. CT9 — 20 C4
Friends Av. CT9 — 20 C5
Fulham Av. CT9 — 18 D5
Fulsam Pl. CT9 — 3 A4

Gainsboro Rd. CT7 — 16 D2
Gainsborough Dr. CT6 — 13 G2
Galliard St. CT13 — 29 F2
Gallwey Av. CT7 — 16 C3
Gann Rd. CT5 — 9 G2
Garden Cl. CT2 — 30 B6
Garfield Rd. CT9 — 3 A4
Garrard Av. CT9 — 18 D4
Gas Pass. CT1 — 6 A5
Gas St. CT1 — 6 A5
Gateacre Rd. CT5 — 8 B5
Genesta Av. CT5 — 8 C4
George Hill Rd. CT10 — 20 D4
George Pk. CT9 — 18 D4
George Roche Rd. CT1 — 35 F4
George St. CT11 — 4 C2
George V Av. CT9 — 18 D4
Georges Av. CT5 — 8 C5
Gilbert Rd. CT11 — 25 E3
Gilchrist Av. CT6 — 11 H4
Giles Gdns. CT9 — 19 G4
Giles La. CT2 — 30 C5
Gillon Mews. CT1 — 31 H6
Gladstone Rd. CT10 — 5 A3
Gladstone Rd. CT5 — 9 E2
Gladstone Rd. CT9 — 19 G4
Glebe Ct. CT12 — 15 B6
Glebe Gdns. CT9 — 18 C5
Glebe Rd. CT9 — 18 C5
Glebe Way. CT5 — 9 E4
Glebelands. CT3 — 27 B2
Glen Av. CT6 — 13 E2
Glen Iris Av. CT2 — 30 C6
Glen Iris Cl. CT2 — 30 C6
Glen Walk. CT5 — 7 A3
Glenbervie Dr. CT6 — 13 G1
Glenbrook Cl. CT6 — 13 F2
Glencoe Rd. CT9 — 19 H3
Glenside. CT5 — 9 H4
Glenside Av. CT1 — 31 H5
Gloucester Av. CT9 — 20 C3
Gloucester Av. CT10 — 23 E5
Gloucester Rd. CT5 — 9 G2
Godden Rd. CT2 — 31 G4
Godwin Rd. CT9 — 20 A3
Godwin Rd. CT1 — 34 C4
Golden Acre La. CT8 — 17 H3
Golden Cl. CT8 — 17 H3
Golden Hill. CT5 — 9 G5
Goldfinch Cl. CT6 — 13 E4
Goodban Sq. CT13 — 27 B2
Goodwin Av. CT5 — 10 C3
Goodwin Rd. CT11 — 24 C5
Gordon Gro. CT8 — 18 A4
Gordon Rd,
  Canterbury. CT1 — 6 A5
Gordon Rd,
  Herne Bay. CT6 — 12 C3
Gordon Rd,
  Margate. CT9 — 19 H2

Gordon Rd,
  Ramsgate. CT11 — 25 E2
Gordon Rd,
  Westwood. CT9 — 22 A3
Gordon Rd,
  Whitstable. CT5 — 9 E4
Gordon Sq. CT7 — 16 D3
Gore End Cl. CT7 — 16 C3
Gore La. CT13 — 27 B5
Gore Mews. CT1 — 31 H6
Gore Rd. CT13 — 27 B5
Gore Ter. CT13 — 27 B5
Goretop La. CT14 — 29 G5
Gorrell Rd. CT5 — 9 F3
Gorse La. CT6 — 13 E5
Gosfield Rd. CT6 — 12 C2
Gosselin St. CT5 — 9 F4
Goudhurst Cl. CT2 — 31 G4
Grafton Rise. CT6 — 11 H2
Grafton Rd. CT10 — 21 E6
Granary Pl. CT5 — 9 E5
Grand Dr. CT6 — 11 G1
Grange Rd. CT11 — 4 A4
Grange Rd. CT6 — 13 E2
Grange Rd. CT10 — 23 E1
Grange Way. CT10 — 23 E6
Grant Cl. CT10 — 23 E2
Granville Av. CT10 — 5 C5
Granville Av. CT11 — 24 C1
Granville Dr. CT6 — 11 G4
*Granville Farm Mews,
  Thanet Rd. CT11 — 25 G3
Granville Rd. CT10 — 5 B5
Grasmere Av. CT11 — 24 B4
Grasmere Rd. CT5 — 9 H3
Gravel Walk. CT1 — 6 C4
Grays Way. CT1 — 34 C4
Graystone Rd. CT5 — 9 H1
Green Acres Cl. CT6 — 12 D4
Green Cloth Mews. CT1 — 31 H6
Green Ct. CT4 — 37 B5
Green Dell. CT2 — 31 F4
Green La. CT5 — 9 E4
Green La. CT9 — 20 D5
Green La. CT10 — 23 E3
Green Leas. CT5 — 10 C5
Green Rd. CT7 — 16 D2
Greenfield Rd. CT12 — 22 C6
Greenhill Bridge Rd.
  CT6 — 11 H2
Greenhill Cl. CT12 — 15 B4
Greenhill Gdns. CT6 — 11 H2
Greenhill Gdns. CT12 — 15 B5
Greenhill Rd. CT6 — 11 G4
Greenhouse La. CT2 — 31 E6
Grenham Bay Av. CT7 — 16 C3
Grenham Rd. CT7 — 16 C2
Grenville Gdns. CT7 — 16 C2
Grenville Way. CT10 — 23 E4
Gresham Av. CT9 — 18 C4
Greville Homes. CT13 — 27 B6
Greystones Rd. CT12 — 26 B5
Grimshill Ct. CT2 — 30 C4
Grimshill Rd. CT5 — 9 F4
Grimthorpe Av. CT5 — 8 D5
Grosvenor Gdns. CT9 — 3 D4
Grosvenor Hill. CT9 — 3 D3
Grosvenor Pl. CT9 — 3 C3
Grosvenor Rd. CT10 — 5 A4
Grosvenor Rd. CT5 — 9 E5
Grosvenor Rd. CT11 — 24 D4
Grotto Gdns. CT9 — 3 F3
Grotto Hill. CT9 — 3 F3
Grotto Rd. CT9 — 3 F2
Grove Gdns. CT9 — 18 D4
Grove Rd. CT11 — 4 B2
Grove Ter. CT1 — 6 A6
Grummock Av. CT11 — 24 C4
Grundys Hill. CT11 — 4 C2
Guildcount La. CT13 — 29 E1
Guildford Av. CT8 — 17 H3
Guildford Lawn. CT11 — 4 C2
Guildford Rd. CT1 — 35 F3
Guildhall St. CT1 — 6 C3
Guilton. CT3 — 27 A2
Guy Cl. CT10 — 23 G1
Gwyn Rd. CT11 — 24 D1
Hackington Cl. CT2 — 31 E4
Hackington Pl. CT2 — 31 F6
Hackington Rd. CT2 — 31 E2
Hackington Ter. CT2 — 31 F6
Hadleigh Gdns. CT6 — 12 D2
Hadlow Dr. CT2 — 21 E3
Haine Ind Est. CT12 — 24 A2
Haine Rd. CT12 — 22 A5

Hales Dr. CT2 — 31 F5
Halfmile Ride. CT9 — 19 F6
Halford Cl. CT6 — 13 E5
Hall-by-the-Sea-Rd. CT9 — 3 B3
Hallcroft Ct. CT11 — 24 D4
Hallett Walk. CT1 — 31 H6
Halstead Cl. CT2 — 31 G4
Halstead Gdns. CT9 — 21 E3
Ham Shades La. CT5 — 9 H3
Hamilton Cl. CT12 — 24 B1
Hamilton Rd. CT5 — 9 F2
Hampshire Rd. CT1 — 36 B3
Hampton Cl. CT6 — 11 F3
Hampton Gdns. CT6 — 11 F3
Hampton Pier Av. CT6 — 11 G2
Hanover Cl. CT9 — 20 D3
Hanover Pl. CT2 — 31 F6
Hanover Sq. CT6 — 12 C2
Hanover St. CT6 — 12 B2
Harbledown By-Pass.
  CT2 — 34 A1
Harbledown Gdns. CT9 — 20 D2
Harbledown Pk. CT2 — 34 C1
Harbour Par. CT11 — 4 D2
Harbour St. CT11 — 4 D2
Harbour St. CT10 — 5 D3
Harbour St. CT5 — 9 E2
Harcourt Dr. CT6 — 11 G1
Harcourt Dr. CT2 — 30 D6
Hardres Rd. CT11 — 25 F3
Hardres St. CT11 — 4 D1
Hardy Cl. CT2 — 34 D1
Harkness Dr. CT2 — 30 D6
Harmsworth Gdns. CT10 — 5 A1
Harnet St. CT13 — 29 E2
Harold Av. CT8 — 18 A4
Harold Rd. CT7 — 16 B2
Harold Rd. CT9 — 20 A3
Harrison Rd. CT11 — 4 A3
Harrow Dene. CT10 — 23 E3
Harry Wells Rd. CT6 — 11 G2
Hartsdown Rd. CT9 — 19 E4
Harvest Rd. CT6 — 13 F5
Harvey Dr. CT5 — 10 A5
Harwich St. CT5 — 9 E4
Hassall Reach. CT1 — 34 B4
Hastings Av. CT9 — 20 A4
Hastings Pl. CT13 — 29 E3
Hatch La. CT4 — 39 C1
Hatfield Rd. CT9 — 3 A3
Hatfield Rd. CT11 — 4 A1
Havelock Pl. CT3 — 27 C2
Havelock St. CT1 — 6 D3
Haven Dr. CT6 — 13 H1
Hawe Cl. CT2 — 31 G4
Hawe Farm Way. CT6 — 12 D5
Hawes Av. CT11 — 24 C4
Hawk Cl. CT5 — 8 D5
Hawkhurst Cl. CT7 — 17 E2
Hawkhurst Way. CT10 — 23 G6
Hawks La. CT1 — 6 B4
Hawks Rd. CT6 — 11 G4
Hawley Sq. CT9 — 3 D3
Hawley St. CT9 — 3 D2
Hawthorn Av. CT2 — 31 G5
Hawthorn Cl. CT11 — 25 E1
Hay Hill. CT13 — 27 D6
Hazelmere Dr. CT6 — 13 F1
Hazelwood Mdw. CT13 — 29 E3
Hazlemere Rd. CT5 — 8 B5
Headcorn Dr. CT2 — 31 G4
Headcorn Gdns. CT9 — 20 D3
Heart In Hand Rd. CT6 — 13 H5
Heath Cl. CT2 — 32 C1
Heather Cl. CT9 — 19 E4
Heathwood Dr. CT9 — 25 F1
Heaton Rd. CT1 — 35 E3
Helding Cl. CT6 — 13 E4
Helena Av. CT9 — 19 G4
Helmdon Cl. CT12 — 22 C6
Helvellyn Av. CT11 — 24 C3
Hengist Av. CT9 — 20 A4
Hengist Rd. CT7 — 16 B3
Hengist Rd. CT8 — 17 H2
Henry Ct. CT1 — 6 B6
Herbert Rd. CT11 — 24 D4
Hereford Gdns. CT7 — 16 D4
Hereson Rd. CT11 — 25 F3
Hereward Av. CT7 — 16 C2
Heritage Cl. CT5 — 8 B6
Herne Av. CT6 — 12 D3
Herne Bay Rd. CT5 — 10 A3
Herne Bay Rd. CT2 — 12 D3
Herne Dr. CT6 — 11 H3
Herne St. CT6 — 14 C1
Herneville Gdns. CT6 — 12 D3

Heronden Rd. CT13 — 27 A6
Herschell Rd. CT7 — 16 D2
Hertford Pl. CT11 — 4 C3
Hertford Rd. CT9 — 20 B5
Hertford St. CT11 — 4 C3
Hever Pl. CT1 — 31 G5
Hibernia St. CT1 — 4 D2
High St, Bridge. CT4 — 37 A4
High St,
  Broadstairs. CT10 — 5 A3
High St,
  Canterbury. CT1 — 6 D2
High St, Eastry. CT13 — 27 B5
High St, Fordwich. CT2 — 32 D4
High St, Garlinge. CT9 — 18 C5
High St,
  Herne Bay. CT6 — 12 B2
High St,
  Littlebourne. CT3 — 38 A2
High St, Manston. CT12 — 26 D3
High St, Margate. CT9 — 3 D3
High St, Minster. CT12 — 15 B5
High St,
  Northgate. CT1 — 35 G1
High St, Ramsgate. CT11 — 4 C1
High St,
  St Lawrence. CT11 — 24 D3
High St, St Peters. CT10 — 23 E3
High St,
  Sandwich. CT13 — 29 F2
High St, Sturry. CT2 — 32 D3
High St, Whitstable. CT5 — 9 E2
High St Par. CT1 — 6 B3
High View Av. CT6 — 11 G1
Higham La. CT4 — 37 C6
Highbury Gdns. CT12 — 22 B5
Highfield Cl. CT12 — 22 B5
Highfield Cl. CT2 — 30 C5
Highfield Gdns. CT9 — 3 A4
Highfield Rd. CT12 — 22 B5
Highfields Vw. CT6 — 13 F2
Highgate Rd. CT5 — 10 A5
Highland Rd. CT4 — 39 B3
Hilary Cl. CT6 — 13 F2
Hildersham Cl. CT10 — 23 E2
Hill Dr. CT13 — 27 B5
Hill House Dr. CT12 — 15 B4
Hill Top Rd. CT6 — 12 D2
Hillborough Dr. CT6 — 13 H1
Hillborough Park. CT6 — 13 H2
Hillborough Rd. CT6 — 13 E2
Hillbrow Av. CT6 — 12 D4
Hillbrow Av. CT2 — 32 D1
Hillbrow Rd. CT11 — 25 E2
Hillcrest Gdns. CT11 — 24 C4
Hillcrest Rd. CT3 — 38 A2
Hillcroft Rd. CT6 — 12 D4
Hiller Cl. CT10 — 23 G2
Hillman Av. CT6 — 11 F2
Hillside Av. CT2 — 30 C6
Hillside Rd. CT5 — 9 H3
Hillview Rd. CT5 — 9 E4
Hillview Rd. CT2 — 30 C6
Hinchliffe Way. CT9 — 20 C5
Hoades Wood Rd. CT2 — 33 E1
Hoath Rd. CT2 — 38 A4
Hobart Rd. CT2 — 24 B1
Hockerdge Gdns. CT8 — 18 B4
Hodges Gap. CT9 — 20 B2
Hodgson Rd. CT5 — 8 A5
Hogarth Cl. CT9 — 13 G2
Hogs Cnr. CT13 — 29 F2
Holbrook Dr. CT11 — 14 D1
Holbrook Dr. CT12 — 24 C1
Holiday Sq. CT9 — 3 D2
Holland Cl. CT10 — 21 G4
Hollicondane Rd. CT11 — 25 E3
Hollow La. CT1 — 35 E4
Hollowmede. CT1 — 35 E4
Holly Cl. CT10 — 22 C4
Holly Cl. CT13 — 22 C4
Holly Gdns. CT9 — 20 C4
Holly La. CT9 — 20 B4
Holly Rd. CT11 — 25 F2
Holm Oak Cl. CT1 — 35 F4
Holm Oak Gdns. CT10 — 23 F4
Holmscroft Rd. CT6 — 13 F2
Holness Rd. CT3 — 27 B1
Holton Cl. CT7 — 17 E5
Home Stead Village.
  CT11 — 24 D5
Homefern Ho. CT9 — 3 D2
Homeleigh Rd. CT12 — 22 B5
Homestall Ct. CT2 — 30 C4
Homewood Rd. CT2 — 32 D2

Honeysuckle Cl. CT9 — 19 E
Honeysuckle Rd. CT11 — 25 G
Honeysuckle Way. CT6 — 13 F
Honeywood Cl. CT1 — 31 H
Honfleur Rd. CT13 — 29 E
Hoopers La. CT6 — 13 F
Hopes La. CT12 — 22 C
Hopeville Av. CT10 — 22 C
Hornet Cl. CT10 — 22 C
Horsa Rd. CT7 — 16 B
Horsebridge Rd. CT5 — 9 E
Hoser Gdns. CT7 — 17 E
Hospital La. CT1 — 6 B
Hovenden Cl. CT2 — 31 G
Howard Rd. CT10 — 5 A
Hubert Way. CT10 — 23 B
Hudson Cl. CT2 — 32 D
Hudson Rd. CT1 — 31 H
Hugin Av. CT10 — 20 D
Humber Av. CT6 — 11 E
Hundreds Cl. CT8 — 17 H
Hunters Chase. CT5 — 9 H
Hunters Chase. CT6 — 13
Hunters Forstal Rd. CT6 — 13 E
Hunting Gate. CT7 — 16 D
Hunton Gdns. CT2 — 31 G
Hurst Gro. CT12 — 24 D
Hythe Pl. CT13 — 29

Iffin La. CT4 — 35
Ince Rd. CT2 — 32 D
INDUSTRIAL ESTATES:.
  All Saints Ind Est. CT9 — 3
  Canterbury Retail Pk.
    CT1 — 32
  City Business Pk. CT1 — 32 A
  Crystal Business
    Centre CT13 — 29 C
  Eddington Business Pk.
    CT6 — 12
  Haine Ind Est CT12 — 24 A
  John Wilson
    Business Pk. CT5 — 10 A
  Joseph Wilson
    Ind Est. CT5 — 9
  St Augustines
    Business Pk. CT5 — 10
  Sandwich Ind Est.
    CT13 — 29 C
  Telegraph Hill Ind Est.
    CT12 — 15 C
  Westwood Ind Est.
    CT9 — 22 A
  Wincheap Ind Est.
    CT1 — 34 D
Ingle Cl. CT7 — 17
Ingoldsby Rd. CT7 — 16
Ingoldsby Rd. CT1 — 34 D
Inverness Ter. CT10 — 5
Invicta Rd. CT5 — 9 C
Invicta Rd. CT9 — 20
Irchester St. CT11 — 4
Iron Bar La. CT1 — 6
Irvine Dr. CT9 — 20
Island Rd. CT2 — 32
Island Rd. CT3 — 38
Island Wall. CT5 — 8
Ivanhoe Rd. CT6 — 12
Ivanhoe Rd. CT8 — 18 A
Ivy House Rd. CT5 — 9 C
Ivy La. CT11 — 4
Ivy La. CT1 — 6
Ivy Pl. CT1 — 35
Ivy Ter. CT1 — 6
Ivychurch Gdns. CT9 — 21

Jackson Rd. CT1 — 35
Jacob Cl. CT9 — 3
James Cl. CT3 — 27
James St. CT11 — 4
Jasmine Cl. CT4 — 39
Jayne Walk. CT5 — 8
Jennifer Gdns. CT9 — 20
*Jessica Mews,
  Military Rd. CT1 — 31
Jesuit Cl. CT2 — 31
Jewry La. CT1 — 6
John St. CT10 — 5
John Wilson
  Business Park. CT5 — 10
Johns Grn. CT13 — 28
*Joseph Conrad Ho,
  Bishops Way. CT2 — 34
Joseph Wilson
  Industrial Estate. CT5 — 9
Joss Gap Rd. CT10 — 21

y La. CT5 8 B5
bilee Ct. CT10 5 C4
bilee Rd. CT13 29 E2
bilee Rd. CT14 29 G6
bilee Rd. CT3 38 A2
lie Cl. CT10 23 F1
nction Rd. CT6 11 G4
niper Cl. CT5 9 G3
niper Cl. CT1 35 G4

eat Farm CT. CT6 13 H2
epers Hill. CT4 37 D3
ith Av. CT12 24 B2
mp Rd. CT5 10 B4
msing Gdns. CT2 31 H4
ndal Cl. CT11 24 C4
ndal Rise. CT10 5 A1
nsington Rd. CT1 32 A4
nt Av. CT1 36 A2
nt Gdns. CT7 16 D3
nt International
Airport. CT12 26 B2
nt Pl. CT11 4 E2
nt Rd. CT9 20 B5
nt St. CT5 9 E4
nt Ter. CT11 4 E2
ntmere Av. CT11 24 A4
nton Gdns. CT12 15 B5
vin Dr. CT11 24 C5
yworth Mews. CT1 31 H6
lbride Cl,
Argyll Dr. CT11 25 G1
ndown Gdns. CT9 20 D3
ndown Gdns. CT14 31 G4
mberley Gro. CT6 8 B6
mberley Rd. CT12 24 B1
ng Arthur Rd. CT12 26 C4
ng Edward Av. CT10 5 B4
ng Edward Av. CT6 13 E2
ng Edward Rd. CT7 16 D5
ng Edward Rd. CT11 24 D4
ng Edward St. CT5 9 E3
ng St. CT9 3 D2
ng St. CT11 4 D2
ng St. CT1 6 C3
ng St. CT13 29 F2
ng St. CT2 32 D4
gfisher Cl. CT5 8 D5
gfisher Cl. CT9 18 C5
gfisher Ct. CT6 12 A4
gfisher Walk. CT10 23 E3
gs Av. CT10 5 B1
gs Av. CT5 9 G3
gs Av. CT7 16 B3
gs Av. CT12 24 C2
gs Pk. CT1 35 H1
gs Rd. CT6 12 B2
gs Rd. CT7 17 E5
gs Rd. CT11 25 G3
gsdown Park. CT5 9 G1
gsfield Rd. CT6 13 E4
gsgate Av. CT10 21 E4
gsgate Bay Rd.
CT10 21 G3
gsley Rd. CT5 9 F4
gsmead Rd. CT11 31 G6
gston Av. CT9 18 D5
gston Cl. CT6 13 H2
gston Cl. CT12 24 C1
bys La. CT2 6 A2
kstone Av. CT11 24 A4
e Farm. CT5 10 C2
ght Av. CT2 34 C2
ghtrider St. CT13 29 F2
ghts Av. CT10 5 C1
ockholt Rd. CT9 21 E2
old Pk. CT9 19 F5
otts La. CT1 6 C2
owler Way. CT6 13 F2
owlton Walk. CT1 31 H6

Belle Alliance Sq.
CT11 4 E1
ournum Av. CT13 29 E3
ournum La. CT2 33 E1
ly Woottons Grn. CT1 6 D3
lyfields. CT6 13 F5
lysmith Gro. CT8 5 B6
lysmith Rd. CT5 7 C2
os Av. CT12 24 B2
eham Gdns. CT9 20 B4
eham Rd. CT9 20 B4
eham Walk. CT9 20 A5
nberhurst Way. CT9 21 E3
nbeth Rd. CT1 32 A4

*Lambourne Wk,
Russett Rd. CT1 36 A2
Lambs Walk. CT5 8 D6
Laming Rd. CT7 17 E4
Lancaster Cl. CT12 24 C1
Lancaster Gdns. CT6 13 G1
Lancaster Gdns. CT7 16 D4
Lancaster Rd. CT1 35 F3
Lanchester Cl. CT6 11 F3
Landon Rd. CT6 13 E2
Lane End. CT6 12 A2
Lanfranc Gdns. CT2 34 C1
Lang Ct. CT5 10 B3
Langdale Av. CT11 24 B4
Langdon Av. CT3 27 D3
Langham Cl. CT9 18 C4
Langley Gdns. CT9 20 D2
Langton La. CT4 35 G6
Lansdown Rd. CT1 6 C6
Lanthorne Rd. CT10 23 F1
Larch Cl. CT2 22 D4
Larkey Vw. CT4 39 C3
Latimer Cl. CT6 11 F3
Laundry Rd. CT12 15 C5
Laureate Cl. CT9 20 B4
Laurel Way. CT4 39 D3
Lauriston Cl. CT11 24 B5
Lauriston Mount. CT10 5 A1
Lausanne Rd. CT9 3 E3
Lavender Cl. CT5 10 B4
Lavender Cl. CT9 19 E4
Lawley Cl. CT12 24 D1
Lawn Rd. CT10 5 A3
Lawn Villas. CT11 4 C2
Lawrence Gdns. CT6 13 E3
Lawson Cl. CT4 39 C3
Laxton Way. CT5 10 B5
Laxton Way. CT1 36 A2
Lay La. CT3 27 C2
Laylam Cl. CT10 22 D3
Leas Grn. CT10 22 D4
Leatt Cl. CT10 23 E4
*Leggetts La,
Sea St. CT5 9 E2
Leicester Av. CT9 20 C3
Leigh Rd. CT12 24 A2
Leighville Dr. CT6 12 A3
Lenham Cl. CT10 23 F6
Lenham Gdns. CT8 18 C5
Leonards Av. CT11 25 F2
Leopold Rd. CT11 25 F2
Leopold St. CT11 4 D2
Lerryn Gdns. CT10 21 E5
Lesley Av. CT1 35 G4
Leslie Av. CT9 18 C5
Leslie Rd. CT7 17 E2
Lewis Cres. CT9 20 A2
Leybourn Rd. CT10 5 C6
Leybourne Dr. CT9 18 C4
Leycroft Cl. CT2 31 E5
Lichfield Av. CT1 35 H4
Lillian Rd. CT11 25 F2
Lime Kiln Rd. CT1 6 B6
Lincoln Av. CT1 35 H3
Lincoln Cl. CT5 10 C2
Lincoln Gdns. CT7 16 D3
Linden Av. CT10 5 C2
Linden Av. CT5 9 G3
Linden Av. CT6 12 A3
Linden Chase. CT2 6 A4
Linden Cl. CT8 18 A5
Linden Gro. CT2 6 A4
Linden Rd. CT8 18 A5
Linden Rd. CT4 39 D3
Lindenthorpe Rd. CT10 5 A3
Lindridge Cl. CT6 14 D1
Linington Rd. CT7 17 E4
Link La. CT1 6 C4
Link Rd. CT10 21 E6
Link Rd. CT2 31 E2
Links Cl. CT6 12 D4
Linksfield Rd. CT8 17 H3
Linley Rd. CT10 23 E1
Linnet Av. CT5 8 D6
Lismore Rd. CT5 10 A6
Lismore Rd. CT6 13 F1
Liss Rd. CT13 27 A6
Lister Rd. CT9 19 H4
*Little Charles St,
Charles St. CT6 12 C1
Little Paddocks CT5 10 C6
Little Walton. CT13 27 C5
Littlebourne Rd. CT3 36 A2
Liverpool Lawn. CT11 4 D3
Livingstone Rd. CT10 23 E2
Lloyd Rd. CT10 5 A3

Lombard St. CT9 3 D2
London Rd. CT11 24 C4
London Rd. CT2 34 D1
Long Acre Cl. CT2 31 E6
Long Dr. CT13 27 C5
Long Meadow Way.
CT2 31 G4
Long Reach Cl. CT5 9 E6
Long Rock. CT5 10 C3
Longacre. CT5 10 C5
Longfield Cl. CT5 10 C3
Longmarket. CT1 6 C4
Longmead Cl. CT6 11 H3
Longport. CT1 6 D4
Longtye Dr. CT5 10 B6
Lonsdale Av. CT9 20 B2
Lonsdale Dr. CT6 11 G1
Loop Ct Mews. CT13 29 E1
Loop St. CT13 29 E2
Lorina Rd. CT12 24 D4
Lorne Rd. CT11 24 D4
Louisa Gap. CT10 5 C5
Love La. CT9 3 D2
Love La. CT1 6 D4
Love St. CT13 29 F2
Love St Cl. CT6 11 H4
Lovell Rd. CT2 30 B5
Lower Bridge St. CT1 6 D4
Lower Chantry La. CT1 35 G2
Lower Gore La. CT13 27 B4
Lower Herne Rd. CT6 12 A6
Lower Northdown Av.
CT9 20 A4
Lower St. CT13 27 C6
Lucerne Dr. CT5 8 A6
Luckhurst Gdns. CT9 20 D3
Luton Av. CT10 5 A5
Luton Ct. CT10 5 A5
Lyell Rd. CT7 16 D3
Lyminge Way. CT9 20 B4
Lymington Rd. CT8 17 H3
Lyndhurst Av. CT9 20 A3
Lyndhurst Cl. CT2 31 E5
Lyndhurst Rd. CT10 5 B3
Lyndhurst Rd. CT11 25 G3
Lyngate Ct. CT9 20 D3
Lypeatt Ct. CT2 30 C3
Lysander Cl. CT10 22 C5
Lytham Av. CT6 12 A5

McCarthy Av. CT2 32 D1
Macdonald Par. CT5 8 B5
Madeira Rd. CT9 19 H2
Madeira Walk. CT11 4 D2
Magdala Rd. CT10 23 E2
Magdalen Cl. CT10 5 B1
Magdalen Ct. CT1 35 G3
Magnolia Av. CT9 20 C3
Magnolia Rise. CT6 13 G5
Maiden La. CT1 34 D4
Mallory Cl. CT12 22 C6
Malthouse Rd. CT2 31 F6
Malvern Pk. CT6 13 F2
Manciple Cl. CT2 34 C2
Mandeville Rd. CT2 31 E6
Manor Cl. CT1 34 C5
Manor Cl. CT6 13 H1
Manor Dr. CT7 16 D4
Manor Lea Rd. CT7 14 C6
Manor Rd. CT10 5 A5
Manor Rd. CT5 9 H1
Manor Rd. CT6 13 H1
Manor Rd. CT7 14 C6
Mansion St. CT9 3 D2
Manston Court Rd. CT9 22 A4
Manston Court Rd.
CT12 22 A4
Manston Pk. CT12 15 C1
Manston Rd,
Birchington. CT7 17 E6
Manston Rd,
Manston. CT12 26 A2
Manston Rd,
Margate. CT9 19 F6
Manston Rd,
Newington. CT12 24 A2
Manwood Av. CT2 31 F4
Manwood Rd. CT13 29 E1
Maple Cl. CT2 30 B5
Maple Ct. CT3 38 C4
Maple Gdns. CT3 38 C4
Marden Av. CT12 24 B6
Margate Hill. CT7 17 G6
Margate Rd,
Broomfield. CT6 13 E4
Margate Rd,

Westwood. CT12 22 A3
Margate Rd,
Whitehall. CT12 24 D1
Marilyn Cres. CT7 17 F3
Marina Esplanade. CT11 4 E2
Marina Rd. CT11 4 F1
Marine Cres. CT5 10 A3
Marine Dr. CT9 3 C3
Marine Dr. CT10 21 F3
Marine Gap. CT5 9 E2
Marine Gdns. CT9 3 C3
Marine Par. CT5 9 G1
Marine Ter. CT9 3 B3
Marine Ter. CT5 8 D2
Maritime Av. CT6 13 E3
Mark Av. CT11 24 C5
Market Pl. CT9 3 D2
Market St. CT9 3 D2
Market St. CT6 12 B1
Market St. CT13 29 F2
Market Way. CT2 31 G6
Marlborough Cl. CT10 23 E5
Marlborough Rd. CT11 4 B2
Marlborough Rd. CT5 7 D1
Marlborough Rd. CT9 19 F4
Marley Ct. CT2 30 C4
Marlow Cl. CT5 10 A4
Marlowe Arc. CT1 6 C4
Marlowe Av. CT1 6 B5
Marlowe Mdws. CT2 32 D3
Marlowe Rd. CT9 20 B5
Marrose Av. CT12 22 B5
Marsh Farm Rd. CT12 15 B6
Marshall Cres. CT10 23 E4
Marshborough Rd.
CT13 28 A3
Marshwood Cl. CT1 32 A5
Martindale Cl. CT1 35 G3
Martindown Rd. CT5 8 D5
Martins Cl. CT12 24 D1
Martyrs Field Rd. CT1 6 A6
Mary Green Walk. CT1 31 H6
Maryland Gro. CT1 35 H4
Masons Rise. CT10 5 A2
Matthews Rd. CT6 11 H4
Maugham Ct. CT5 9 E4
Maxine Gdns. CT10 23 E3
May St. CT6 13 H3
Maydowns Rd. CT5 10 C4
Mayfield Rd. CT6 12 C3
Mayforth Rd. CT11 24 C5
Maynard Av. CT9 18 D5
Maynard Rd. CT1 35 E3
Mays Rd. CT11 24 D4
Mayville Rd. CT10 23 E2
Mead Way. CT2 35 E1
Meadow Cl. CT6 13 E3
Meadow Cl. CT4 37 C5
Meadow Dr. CT5 10 C5
Meadow Rd,
Canterbury. CT2 30 C6
Meadow Rd,
Garlinge. CT9 18 C4
Meadow Rd,
Sturry. CT2 32 D2
Meadow Walk. CT5 8 D5
Medina Av. CT5 8 C5
Meeting St. CT11 4 C1
Melbourne Av. CT12 24 C1
Mellanby Cl. CT7 17 E4
Melsetter Cl. CT7 17 F3
Melville Lea. CT13 28 B4
Memel Pl. CT11 4 B2
Mentmore Rd. CT12 22 C5
Mercery La. CT1 6 C3
Merchants Way. CT2 34 C2
Mere Gate. CT9 19 F4
Merrywood Gro. CT6 13 F5
Merton La. CT4 35 E6
Metcalfe Mews. CT1 31 H6
Meteor Av. CT5 8 C4
Meverall Av. CT12 26 C5
Michael Av. CT11 25 G2
Michelle Gdns. CT9 18 B4
Mickleburgh Av. CT6 12 D3
Mickleburgh Hill. CT6 12 C2
Middle Wall. CT5 9 E2
Miles Way. CT7 16 D3
Military Rd. CT11 4 C3
Military Rd. CT1 6 D2
Mill Bank Cotts. CT13 27 A6
Mill Cl. CT13 28 D1
Mill Cotts. CT11 4 A3
Mill Field. CT10 23 F2
Mill Fld. CT2 27 D3
Mill Grn. CT13 27 B6

Mill La. CT9 3 D3
Mill La. CT1 6 C2
Mill La. CT6 12 D5
Mill La. CT7 16 D4
Mill La. CT13 27 A6
Mill La. CT2 34 C2
Mill La. CT4 37 A5
Mill La Nth. CT6 13 E4
Mill Rd. CT2 32 C3
Mill Row. CT7 16 D4
Mill Ter, Bridge. CT4 37 A5
Mill Ter,
Chartham. CT4 39 C1
Mill View Rd. CT6 12 C5
Miller Av. CT2 34 D1
Millers Ct. CT5 9 E5
Millfield Manor. CT5 9 F3
Millfield Rd. CT12 22 B5
Millmead Av. CT9 20 C5
Millmead Gdns. CT9 20 C4
Millmead Rd. CT9 20 A4
Millstream Cl. CT5 9 F3
Millstrood Rd. CT5 9 F3
Millwall Pl. CT13 29 F2
Milner La. CT2 32 C3
Milner Rd. CT5 8 B6
Milton Av. CT9 3 E4
Milton Cl. CT1 36 A4
Milton Rd. CT5 35 G4
Milton Sq. CT9 3 E4
Minnis Rd. CT7 16 B2
Minnis Way. CT14 29 G6
Minster Cl. CT10 23 G6
Minster Dr. CT6 12 A2
Minster Rd. CT12 15 B1
Minster Rd. CT8 18 A5
Minster Rd. CT11 24 C5
Moat La. CT3 27 C2
Moat La. CT2 32 D4
Moat Sole. CT13 29 E2
Mockett Dr. CT10 21 E6
Molehill Rd. CT5 10 C6
Molehill Rd. CT6 11 E5
Molineux Rd. CT12 15 B6
Molland Cl. CT3 27 B2
Molland La. CT3 27 A2
Molland Lea. CT3 27 B2
Monastery St. CT1 6 D4
Monks Cl. CT2 31 G5
Monkton Gdns. CT9 21 E2
Monkton Pl. CT11 4 C1
Monkton Rd. CT12 15 A5
Montague Rd. CT11 25 F3
Montague St. CT6 12 A2
Montefiore Av. CT11 25 G1
*Montefiore Cotts,
Hereson Rd. CT11 25 G3
Montfort Cl. CT2 31 G4
Montpelier Av. CT5 9 E6
Moorfield. CT2 31 F4
Moray Av. CT7 16 D2
Mordaunt Av. CT8 17 H2
Morris Av. CT6 11 E2
Mortimer St. CT6 12 C1
Moss End Mews. CT11 23 E6
*Mount Charles Wk,
Union Rd. CT4 37 A5
Mount Green Av. CT12 26 C6
Mount Pleasant. CT2 30 A2
Mount Rd. CT1 36 A4
Mount View Rd. CT6 12 D5
Mountfield Way. CT8 17 G4
Moyes Cl. CT12 26 B5
Muir Rd. CT11 25 G2
Mulberry Cl. CT11 25 G3
Mulberry Fld. CT13 29 E1
Musgrave Cl. CT12 26 A2
Mutrix Gdns. CT9 18 C4
Mutrix Rd. CT9 18 C4
Mymms Cl. CT5 10 B6
Mystole La. CT4 39 C3

Nacholt Cl. CT5 9 H2
Nackington La. CT4 35 H6
Nackington Rd. CT1 35 H5
Napier Rd. CT12 23 E2
Napleton Rd. CT11 24 D4
Nargate Cl. CT3 38 B2
Nargate St. CT3 38 B2
Nash Court Gdns. CT9 19 G5
Nash Court Rd. CT9 19 G5
Nash Gdns. CT9 5 C3
Nash La. CT9 19 G5
Nash Rd, Margate. CT9 19 F5
Nash Rd,
Westwood. CT9 22 A3

44

46

ESTATE PUBLICATIONS

LOCAL RED BOOKS

ALFRETON, BELPER, RIPLEY
ASHFORD, TENTERDEN
BANGOR, CAERNARFON
BARNSTAPLE, ILFRACOMBE
BASILDON, BILLERICAY
BASINGSTOKE, ANDOVER
BATH, BRADFORD-ON-AVON
BEDFORD
BOURNEMOUTH, POOLE, CHRISTCHURCH
BRENTWOOD
BRIGHTON, LEWES, NEWHAVEN, SEAFORD
BRISTOL
BROMLEY (London Bromley)
BURTON-UPON-TRENT, SWADLINCOTE
BURY ST. EDMUNDS
CAMBRIDGE
CARDIFF
CHELMSFORD, BRAINTREE, MALDON, WITHAM
CHESTER
CHESTERFIELD
CHICHESTER, BOGNOR REGIS
COATBRIDGE, AIRDRIE
COLCHESTER, CLACTON
CORBY, KETTERING
CRAWLEY & MID SUSSEX
CREWE
DERBY, HEANOR, CASTLE DONINGTON
EASTBOURNE, BEXHILL, SEAFORD, NEWHAVEN
EDINBURGH, MUSSELBURGH, PENICUIK
EXETER, EXMOUTH
FALKIRK, GRANGEMOUTH
FAREHAM, GOSPORT
FLINTSHIRE TOWNS
FOLKESTONE, DOVER, DEAL & ROMNEY MARSH
GLASGOW, & PAISLEY
GLOUCESTER, CHELTENHAM
GRAVESEND, DARTFORD
GRAYS, THURROCK
GREAT YARMOUTH, LOWESTOFT
GRIMSBY, CLEETHORPES
GUILDFORD, WOKING
HAMILTON, MOTHERWELL, EAST KILBRIDE
HARLOW, BISHOPS STORTFORD
HASTINGS, BEXHILL, RYE
HERTFORD, HODDESDON, WARE
HIGH WYCOMBE
HUNTINGDON, ST. NEOTS
IPSWICH, FELIXSTOWE
ISLE OF WIGHT TOWNS
KIDDERMINSTER
KINGSTON-UPON-HULL
LANCASTER, MORECAMBE
LEICESTER, LOUGHBOROUGH
LINCOLN
LLANDUDNO, COLWYN BAY
LUTON, DUNSTABLE
MAIDSTONE
MANSFIELD, MANSFIELD WOODHOUSE
MEDWAY, GILLINGHAM
MILTON KEYNES
NEW FOREST TOWNS
NEWPORT, CHEPSTOW
NEWTOWN, WELSHPOOL
NORTHAMPTON
NORTHWICH, WINSFORD
NORWICH
NOTTINGHAM, EASTWOOD, HUCKNALL, ILKESTON
OXFORD, ABINGDON
PENZANCE, ST. IVES
PETERBOROUGH
PLYMOUTH, IVYBRIDGE, SALTASH, TORPOINT
PORTSMOUTH, HAVANT, WATERLOOVILLE
READING
REDDITCH, BROMSGROVE
REIGATE, BANSTEAD, LEATHERHEAD, DORKING
RHYL, PRESTATYN
RUGBY
ST. ALBANS, WELWYN, HATFIELD

SALISBURY, AMESBURY, WILTON
SCUNTHORPE
SEVENOAKS
SHREWSBURY
SITTINGBOURNE, FAVERSHAM, ISLE OF SHEPPEY
SLOUGH, MAIDENHEAD, WINDSOR
SOUTHAMPTON, EASTLEIGH
SOUTHEND-ON-SEA
STAFFORD
STEVENAGE, HITCHIN, LETCHWORTH
STIRLING
STOKE-ON-TRENT
STROUD, NAILSWORTH
SWANSEA, NEATH, PORT TALBOT
SWINDON, CHIPPENHAM, MARLBOROUGH
TAUNTON, BRIDGWATER
TELFORD
THANET, CANTERBURY, HERNE BAY, WHITSTABLE
TORBAY (Torquay, Paignton, Newton Abbot)
TRURO, FALMOUTH
TUNBRIDGE WELLS, TONBRIDGE, CROWBOROUGH
WARWICK, ROYAL LEAMINGTON SPA &
    STRATFORD UPON AVON
WATFORD, HEMEL HEMPSTEAD
WELLINGBOROUGH
WESTON-SUPER-MARE, CLEVEDON
WEYMOUTH, DORCHESTER
WINCHESTER, NEW ARLESFORD
WORCESTER, DROITWICH
WORTHING, LITTLEHAMPTON, ARUNDEL
WREXHAM

COUNTY RED BOOKS (Town Centre Maps)

BEDFORDSHIRE
BERKSHIRE
BUCKINGHAMSHIRE
CAMBRIDGESHIRE
CHESHIRE
CORNWALL
DERBYSHIRE
DEVON
DORSET
ESSEX
GLOUCESTERSHIRE
HAMPSHIRE
HEREFORDSHIRE
HERTFORDSHIRE
KENT
LEICESTERSHIRE & RUTLAND
NORFOLK
NORTHAMPTONSHIRE
NOTTINGHAMSHIRE
SHROPSHIRE
SOMERSET
STAFFORDSHIRE
SUFFOLK
SURREY
SUSSEX (EAST)
SUSSEX (WEST)
WILTSHIRE
WORCESTERSHIRE

OTHER MAPS

KENT TO CORNWALL (1:460,000)
COUNTY MAP - DORSET
              - SOMERSET
              - WILTSHIRE
CHINA (1:6,000,000)
INDIA (1:3,750,000)
INDONESIA (1:4,000,000)
NEPAL (1,800,000)
SOUTH EAST ASIA (1:6,000,000)
THAILAND (1:1,600,000)

STREET PLANS

EDINBURGH TOURIST PLAN
ST. ALBANS

OFFICIAL TOURIST & LEISURE MAPS

SOUTH EAST ENGLAND (1:200,000)
KENT & EAST SUSSEX (1:150,000)
SUSSEX & SURREY (1:150,000)
SOUTHERN ENGLAND (1:200,000)
ISLE OF WIGHT (1:50,000)
WESSEX (1:200,000)
DEVON & CORNWALL (1:200,000)
CORNWALL (1:180,000)
DEVON (1:200,000)
DARTMOOR & SOUTH DEVON COAST (1:100,000)
EXMOOR & NORTH DEVON COAST (1:100,000)
GREATER LONDON (1:80,000)
GREATER LONDON M25 (1:80,000)
EAST ANGLIA (1:200,000)
CHILTERNS & THAMES VALLEY (1:200,000)
THE COTSWOLDS (1:110,000)
COTSWOLDS & WYEDEAN (1:200,000)
WALES (1:250,000)
CYMRU (1:250,000)
THE SHIRES OF MIDDLE ENGLAND (1:250,000)
STAFFORDSHIRE & SHROPSHIRE (1:200,000)
PEAK DISTRICT (1:100,000)
SNOWDONIA (1:125,000)
YORKSHIRE (1:200,000)
YORKSHIRE DALES (1:125,000)
NORTH YORKSHIRE MOORS (1:125,000)
NORTH WEST ENGLAND (1:200,000)
ISLE OF MAN (1:60,000)
NORTH PENNINES & LAKES (1:200,000)
LAKE DISTRICT (1:75,000)
BORDERS OF ENGLAND & SCOTLAND (1:200,000)
BURNS COUNTRY (1:200,000)
HEART OF SCOTLAND (1:200,000)
GREATER GLASGOW (1:150,000)
EDINBURGH & THE LOTHIANS (1:150,000)
ISLE OF ARRAN (1:63,360)
FIFE (1:100,000)
LOCH LOMOND & TROSSACHS (1:150,000)
ARGYLL THE ISLES & LOCH LOMOND (1:275,000)
PERTHSHIRE, DUNDEE & ANGUS (1:150,000)
FORT WILLIAM, BEN NEVIS, GLEN COE (1:185,00)
IONA (1:10,000) & MULL (1:115,000)
GRAMPIAN HIGHLANDS (1:185,000)
LOCH NESS & INVERNESS (1:150,000)
AVIEMORE & SPEY VALLEY (1:150,000)
SKYE & LOCHALSH (1:130,000)
ARGYLL & THE ISLES (1:200,000)
CAITHNESS & SUTHERLAND (1:185,000)
HIGHLANDS OF SCOTLAND (1:275,000)
WESTERN ISLES (1:125,000)
ORKNEY & SHETLAND (1:128,000)
ENGLAND & WALES (1:650,000)
SCOTLAND (1:500,000)
HISTORIC SCOTLAND (1:500,000)
SCOTLAND CLAN MAP (1:625,000)
BRITISH ISLES (1:1,100,000)
GREAT BRITAIN (1:1,100,000)

EUROPEAN LEISURE MAPS

EUROPE (1:3,100,000)
BENELUX (1:600,000)
FRANCE (1:1,000,000)
GERMANY (1:1,000,000
IRELAND (1:625,000)
ITALY (1:1,000,000)
SPAIN & PORTUGAL (1,1,000,000)
CROSS CHANNEL VISITORS' MAP (1:530,000)
WORLD (1:35,000,000)
WORLD FLAT

TOWNS IN NORTHERN FRANCE STREET ATLAS
BOULOGNE SHOPPERS MAP
CALAIS SHOPPERS MAP
DIEPPE SHOPPERS MAP

ESTATE PUBLICATIONS are also
Distributors in the UK for:

INTERNATIONAL TRAVEL MAPS, Canada
HALLWAG, Switzerland
ORDNANCE SURVEY

Catalogue and prices from:

ESTATE PUBLICATIONS
Bridewell House, Tenterden, Kent. TN30 6EP.

Tel: 01580 764225   Fax: 01580 763720